WRITING AND RIGHTING

LYNDSEY STONEBRIDGE

WRITING AND RIGHTING

Literature in the Age of
Human Rights

OXFORD

UNIVERSITY PRESS

Great Clarendon Street, Oxford, OX2 6DP,
United Kingdom

Oxford University Press is a department of the University of Oxford.
It furthers the University's objective of excellence in research, scholarship,
and education by publishing worldwide. Oxford is a registered trade mark of
Oxford University Press in the UK and in certain other countries

Published in the United States of America by Oxford University Press
198 Madison Avenue, New York, NY 10016, United States of America

British Library Cataloguing in Publication Data
Data available

Library of Congress Control Number: 2020937514

ISBN 978–0–19–881405–4

Printed and bound in Great Britain by
Clays Ltd, Elcograf S.p.A.

For the new people,
my students,
and for Mizzy and Joe Heap and their friends.

PREFACE AND ACKNOWLEDGEMENTS

There are inspiring books that show how the greats of literature teach us about the love and compassion we need to create societies of human rights. This is not one of those books. We
often hear the argument that what is urgently required just now is
more empathy. Literature is a particularly good thing in this
regard, it is said, because reading generates the empathetic feelings
required to develop the kinds of moral imagination that can connect us with the suffering of others. Perhaps this is true. The problem is not simply that too few people are feeling wretched about
the pain of other people or, indeed, that they are not reading.
Levels of troubled sadness in the world are difficult to measure,
but are probably pretty constant. Whilst the mechanics of reading
have changed—we no longer read scrolls, we scroll—the appetite
for words and stories has not. The problem is that for all the reading and all the feeling, the dumping on the powerless by the
powerful has continued. Just lately, many would say, oppression
has got a good deal less shameless.

Human rights are not things we magnanimously grant other
people because we feel bad about how they live. They are
active, contested, and usually political claims for freedom, self-
determination, and protection. Human rights belong to the big
scripts of collective endeavour: to the law; to ideologies and
philosophies of justice and equality; to the books, thinkers,

revolutionaries, artists, activists, and survivors who wanted not just more compassionate feeling in the world, but change, real change. Somewhere along the line, we stopped thinking about creative writing as part of this tradition. A more modest literary humanitarianism crept into our discussions. As for the new readers of the eighteenth-century sentimental novel, books make us feel better about the world. Feeling better, of course, might also mean feeling more thoughtfully, more attuned to gross inequality and the multiple moral ironies of feeling so bad about powerlessness whilst keeping so much power, for example. But it may not.

The chapters collected in this small book are inspired by writers for whom empathy is not enough.[1] Virginia Woolf, Behrouz Boochani, Suzanne Césaire, Simone Weil, Samuel Beckett, Kamila Shamsie, Ben Okri, Yousif M. Qasmiyeh, Hannah Arendt—none are content with the terms that liberal human rights handed down to us from the twentieth century. Often writing directly from contexts of rightlessness, all are human rights dissenters as well as defenders, critical-creative moralists who insist, in different ways, that the contemporary project of claiming human dignity is far from complete: indeed, that it has hardly begun.

These are not conducive times for the return of big emancipatory ideas about freedom and equality. Human rights are in retreat. Progressive politics are under direct attack across the globe. But perhaps it is not utopias we need, or fine words about humanity fluttering prettily over the barbed wire. In a world in which there is a market for everything, except for a love without markets, the writers we need most are those who understand, often by necessity, that to write is to claim a way of living and being with others in the world. Writing 'confers—and withdraws—meaning or sense upon a life,' Susan Sontag noted in her final essay (on South African novelist Nadine Gordimer). To write is 'to know something,' which is why to read is an education in moral judgement—it is to respond not merely to the suffering, but to the political and historical claims of others.[2]

Teaching her students about political responsibility in the late twentieth century, Hannah Arendt was careful to distinguish between empathy and moral judgement. Do not fall into the trap, she warned them, of believing you can inhabit the minds, lives, and feelings of others. This is merely to 'swap one passivity for another.' Judgement, rather, means moving and thinking between viewpoints. As Kant put it, a moral imagination is one that has 'trained itself to go visiting.' Judging, for Arendt, as for Kant, was inherently social and political. We cannot judge alone. There's no point in shouting 'but I don't like this, it's bad, ugly, and wrong' into a flickering screen if there is nobody there to like your dislike. Judgement is the middle term between theory and practice, between thought and action, between passivity and active change—between enlightenment and revolution.[3]

It is no coincidence that Arendt liked to teach her students about judgement and politics by getting them to read literature. Over a third of the texts she set on her courses on 'Political Experience' were modern novels, plays or poems. In a reverse move, the first three chapters in this book began on a course I co-taught on literature and human rights in the 2010s, alongside the eighteenth-century literature scholar Ross Wilson. We were teaching literature students to think about the history of human rights through novels, plays, and poems. Working against the backdrop of the war on terror, the rise of ethno-nationalism, the increased marketization of higher education, the return of deten-tion camps for refugees and migrants, the climate emergency, and an ever-diminishing sense of hope for their futures, it would be fair to describe the students on this course as morally restless. Many jibbed against the requirement to package their reading into the canons and methodologies by which the discipline of literary criticism can be judged to have been taught and examined as advertised. They had chosen the course because they had an intuition that literature lived in the world: that it had something to do with us being here together, with right and wrong, with human dignity and human complexity. They certainly were not studying human rights to make themselves feel more helpless in a perplexing and shamelessly unequal world. Nor were they reading books hoping to become nicer human beings. They wanted to join literary communities of empowerment and solidarity, to understand and give meaning to the unexpectedly dismal times they found themselves in.

It is to those students that I owe the fact that this book often breaks with the habits of disinterested theorizing required by my training and profession to, instead, very interestedly affirm the critical human rights work that writing does. This isn't idealism. I understand that that the ways in which literature is world-making more often than not helps make the world in the interests of the powerful. That is precisely why we need to be more suspicious of the claim that literature is a primarily a sentimental education. To cast literature as the cultural wing of a politically impotent humanitarianism is to undersell both human rights and writing as powerful, and sometimes effective, ideas and practises of moral and political being in the world. We are currently living with some of the consequences of that devaluation.

Literature re-creates the experience of the powerless as well as of history's makers—that is another reason why Arendt insisted that her political science students read fiction, poems, and memoirs. We can respond to that powerlessness with pity, and we can measure our democracies' humanism by our capacities for compassion and sympathy. Or we can truly attempt to look upon the world from the perspective of the powerless. The latter is infinitely more difficult because it means acknowledging both that the inequalities and injustices of the world are, in fact, intolerable, and that most of us are implicated in them.[4] To create literary forms in which it is possible to bear this knowledge is a step towards reclaiming human dignity. Acting on that knowledge is another.

*   *   *

Conversations with the following friends and colleagues echo through these essays: Anna Barnard, Julia Bell, Les Back, Hadji Bakara, Homi K. Bhabha, Sarah Churchwell, Bob Eaglestone, Elena Fiddian-Qasmiyeh, Brian Goodman, Shaun Hargreaves Heap, Joe Heap, Laurie Herring, Marianne Hirsch, Stephen Hopgood, Thomas Keenan, Dennis Kennedy, Seraphima Kennedy, Clive Lewis, Gail Lewis, Itamar Mann, Jean McNeil, Rachel Potter, Yousif M. Qasmiyeh, Hari Reed, David Rieff, Michael Rothberg, Rick Rylance, Philippe Sands, Debarati Sanyal, Nando Sigona, Joseph Slaughter, Christopher Smith, and Ross Wilson. Kayvan Tahmasebian provided expert translation from the Persian, and Jess Farr-Cox helped put the book together. Jacqueline Norton, again, was the most patient and amenable of editors. My thanks to Ben Okri and Yousif M. Qasmiyeh for permission to quote from their poems, and to Homa Katouzian for his translation of Saadi. An early version of 'Once More with Feeling' was first published in *The New Humanist* in June 2017. 'Words of Fire' began as an opinion piece in *Open Democracy* in July 2017 and was developed as a keynote for the *Creative Interruptions: A Festival of Arts and Activism* held at the South Bank Centre, London, in May 2019. A short version of 'The Bewilderment of Everyday Violence' was published online in *Prospect UK* in March 2019 and was also a talk given as part of the British Academy's *Experiencing Violence* project. 'Human Time/Survival Time' was written as a keynote for the *Narratives of Forced Migration* conference in Stirling, in September 2019. My thanks to editors and organizers, especially Fiona Barclay, Stephanie Boland, Churnjeet Mahn, Sarita Malik, Beatrice Ivey, Benjamin Ramm, and Daniel Trilling.

TABLE OF CONTENTS

CHAPTER ONE

INTRODUCTION— LITERATURE IN THE ENDTIMES (?) OF HUMAN RIGHTS

There was a time, not too long ago, when it did not seem necessary to describe the relationship between literature and human rights. The connections between the self-evident humanity of books and the bigger project of securing humanity seemed obvious. In many ways, they still are. We read books because they give us blueprints for the ways in which it might be possible to live with others in the world. We write declarations and protocols, endow international courts with power, train legislators and advocates because we also believe it is possible to create legal fictions strong enough to make living with others morally tolerable, if not just.

For much of the post-war period, the activities of discerning humanity through literature and scripting it for a better world were tacitly assumed to be part of a literary education. The new and practical critics of the mid-twentieth century disinterestedly analysed the complexities of the human condition because they valued it. Later, theorists challenged that supposed disinterestedness by arguing that marginalized and more contradictory ways of being were also valuable. And if the knowledge that the writers of every document of humanity had dipped their ink in barbarism always hovered uncomfortably in the background, few in either generation would have dreamt they were doing anything other than supporting the development of human rights with their reading, if only vaguely and non-committedly.

If that assumption has changed, this is because not much about either human rights or the humanizing benefits of a literary education seems self-evident right now.

Modern human rights emerged from three interrelated histories: the total war and genocides of the Second World War; the political and creative struggles of decolonization; and the ideological battles of the Cold War. Each of these intertwined histories has several literary histories too. From anti-colonial poetics to the postcolonial novel; from eye-watering levels of state investment in literature during the Cold War to the marketing of World Literature in the global glory days of neoliberalism; from Holocaust testimony to the *samizdat* underground literary networks, writing has always given expression to the many and often contradictory freedoms of human rights. Up until fairly recently, just as books, by and large, are considered all-round good things, human rights were viewed as a capacious umbrella under which progressives, liberals, pacifists, anti-racists, feminists, anti-colonialists, democratic socialists, internationalists and anti-communists could huddle, albeit in not exactly comfortable proximity.

The one freedom everybody seemed to agree on was freedom of conscience, which is why the symbol of human rights has so often been the pen. The first strategy launched by Amnesty when it was founded in 1961 was a letter writing campaign. It was well-chosen. Writing letters to prisoners of conscience was a way of showing your solidarity by exercising your own conscience: you wrote your own letter, because you were also defending the rights of other people to author their own lives. It was an ethos that was to characterize the development of human rights through the 1970s and 1980s.

But in the years following the end of the Cold War disenchantment began to set in, at least in the West—elsewhere, the enchantment had always been more qualified. What Susan Marks has described as the 'myth of no politics' had made human rights manipulable.[1] Struggles against oppression continued, but, as it became more difficult to disentangle political morality from *realpolitik*, the language of human rights filtered across from local politics, activists, NGOs, writers, and intellectuals and into foreign policy and increasingly centralized humanitarian initiatives. By the late 1990s and early 2000s, it seemed to many that the once capacious umbrella of human rights had snapped shut and was being reemployed as a weapon with which the United States and its allies might re-script the moral and political ordering of the world. Not only did the West appear to think it owned human rights, it was also, on more than a few occasions, proving to be spectacularly bad at them.

Bodged humanitarian operations and an excess of administrative reason appeared to produce nearly as much suffering as it eased. Human rights and humanitarian agencies kept on hearing the words 'development' and 'sustainability', even as many explained that what they also wanted was equality, liberty and justice. The bitter lesson that force always arrived too late to prevent genocide had to be learned twice, first in Bosnia and then in Rwanda. Once learned, however, in practice it proved difficult to keep intervention humanitarian. Actively and responsibly

3

aiming to protect human life by whatever means possible was one thing, but sending over a drone to show how much you cared was another. Or was it? By the time evidence of torture and 'legal black holes' emerged from the second Gulf War, it was becoming difficult to tell what was a blurred line and what a political lie.

At this point, Western writers and scholars from the humanities started looking more critically at their relation to human rights. They did so, in part, to reclaim human rights from the bad history that was building up around them. Historian Lynn Hunt's influential book *Inventing Human Rights* (2007), for example, showed how the revolutionary idea of a shared humanity grew to the extent that torture became more repugnant in the eighteenth century than it seemed to be to many Americans in the early twenty-first.[2] Other historians, such as Samuel Moyn in *The Last Utopia* (2010), subjected the mythologies of the more recent history of human rights to less flattering critique.[3] In literary studies, scholars tracked genealogies of human rights narratives, be they the self-justifications and rhetorical moral hazing of perpetrators and beneficiaries, the Quixotic passions of the humanitarian helper, or the testimonies of victims who, deprived of rights, have more reason than most to create new languages for justice.[4] Deconstructive critics had previously emphasized how the traumatized testimonies of victims shattered systems of moral, political, and legal representation. By the time Baghdad was razed in 2003, the mood was more critically self-reflective: the shattering of international law and the traumatizing of politics had become grotesquely real.[5]

Literature has always been a strong co-creator of ideas about humanity and justice.[6] Eighteenth-century moral philosophers preached the values of sympathetic reason, but as Hunt argued in her book, it was through the novel that the intimate lives of strangers found a place in the hearts of the new middle-classes. The development of the lyric voice in poetry similarly revealed a unique individual, by turns vulnerable and voluble, unafraid to climb above the treeline of the mountains in search of freedom. Historical leaps in the bid for human equality invariably come with innovations in form, genre, and literary expression. Had Jefferson simply repeated 'Let's Get Independence Done' *ad nauseum* (the slogan for the United Kingdom's 2019 election was 'Get Brexit Done') or 'Make America Great', rather than crafting a story about a bad father-king and a different future for his justly rebellious children, things might have worked out differently. Had Frederick Douglass not forged a new genre that defined modern freedom in opposition to colonial slavery in his 1845 memoir *Narrative of the Life of Frederick Douglass, American Slave,* the testimonial form might have ended up merely being supplicatory rather than emancipatory. Had George Orwell not imagined a man restless enough to steal a pen and begin to write down his own thoughts in *Nineteen Eighty-Four* (1949), the totalitarian mind might have remained a theoretical abstraction. And so on. The problem with this progressive view of what literature can do is, of course, that in the round we don't seem to have progressed nearly far enough.

A more sceptical view embraces the idea that literature was—and is—a strong co-creator in ideas about rights and justice, but argues for a bumpier, and possibly in the end more creative, understanding of how human rights get to be imagined and re-imagined in response to different historical and political pressure points. This was an argument first suggested by the philosopher Richard McKeon, who sat on a special Philosophers' Committee convened by UNESCO in 1947 to inquire into the Theoretical Bases of Human Rights. McKeon argued that human rights would never get going at all if we waited for philosophers and legislators to agree about those theoretical foundations. What was required, rather, was simply a universal acknowledgement that human rights existed, albeit in various and relative forms, and to note that this contingency is their historical condition—and, indeed, that contingency might well be their strength. 'The history of human rights must be rewritten, at every stage of its progress, from the point of view of ideas and values, the philosophy, of that period,' he later wrote.[7]

Philosophers and historians have long argued about the origins of human rights. Theories of rights, law, morality, sympathy, dignity, love, and friendship have always been entangled with the messes of political power, sovereignty, capitalism, occupation, and colonialism. Literature occupies the mid-line between the desire to know about how the world might or should be of philosophers, and the realities about what actually happens that concern historians.

Writers have no problem with the idea of rewriting the history of human rights from the point of view of ideas and values that matter to them in their own time. From Leo Tolstoy to Toni Morrison, George Eliot to Primo Levi, Gabriel Garcia Marquez to Mahmoud Darwish, Virginia Woolf to Behrouz Boochani, the most creative political-moralists of their times were never doing anything less.

The legal theorist Martti Koskenniemi has suggested that, given the difficulties of grounding human rights in faith or philosophy, we should instead think about them as 'part of the normative organization' of a period.[8] Writers, we could add, have often been in the vanguard of setting out how political communities wish to judge themselves—and others. Novels invite us into worlds that are enough like the ones we live in to reveal what is beautiful and what is ugly about our lives together. Drama teaches us about the caprice of political fate, the comedy of moral error, and how it is that one person's tragedy can affect everyone. Poetry shares with us the intimacy, weirdness, and dignity of the human mind. There are plenty of super-creative civilizations that never had anything like human rights; what is less clear is whether modern human rights would have been invented without the arts.

This all sounds cute until you remember that there are periods in which it is quite possible for societies to re-organize their norms in opposition to human rights, such as, for instance, now. When I was appointed as a professor of humanities and human rights at the University of Birmingham in 2018, my new colleague, the migration and citizenship expert Nando Sigona, joked (seriously) that the 'human rights' part of my job was redundant before I had even started. He meant this in two senses. On the one hand, the euphoric attacks on human rights from the new right-wing nationalist international (Bolsonaro, Orbán, Erdogan, Trump, Netanyahu, Modi, Putin, Duterte *et al.*) are a clear and direct existential threat to both the idea of human rights and, even more seriously, to the institutions that make them possible, such as courts, treaties, universities, NGOs, and international bodies. But he also meant that human rights had weakened themselves.

In 2013, Stephen Hopgood published an important book entitled *The Endtimes of Human Rights* in which he argued that the West's owning of human rights as a moral project, with its frequently disastrous and unaccountable overreach, was fast approaching its last days.[9] Human rights might survive but only if their so-called moral guardians in the West withdrew, and allowed for their re-writing to continue in other contexts. Any hope of a new times for human rights, Hopgood concluded, rested with local activism and the transnational solidarities—and humanisms—that emerge in response to human suffering and disaster.

At the beginning of the 2020s, humanitarians working in the Mediterranean, Europe, Syria, Iran, China and elsewhere are routinely criminalized. Regimes have re-discovered the populist pleasures to be gained by publicly stripping people of their citizenship (last seen in the late 1930s). Mass bombing, chemical warfare, and genocide have been enabled by bumbling and conveniently supine political elites, whilst, on the borders of Europe and the United States, children lose their minds in refugee and migrant detention camps. And this is all before we can even begin to take stock of the damage done to human life and liberty by responses to COVID 19 (which emerged just as this book went to press). We know we are witnessing major and repeated 'human rights crises' because the media tell us so. But if the word 'crises' obscures the political causes of this suffering, neither are we quite sure that the words 'human rights' any longer carry enough moral, political, cultural, social, or even semantic weight to adequately convey what it is that so many are currently determinedly, urgently, and sometimes desperately working to protect across the globe just now.

Writers are used to words failing. Literary history is good at tracking the mixed moral and political fortunes of language, the moments when, for instance, words such as 'exile' lost their 'tone of sacred awe' and started to 'provoke the idea of something simultaneously suspicious and unfortunate'—the example is Hannah Arendt's from 1944.[10] In better times, other words, such as equality, freedom, and dignity, become part of a culture's normative organization, partly by finding new literary forms. The philosopher Jacques Rancière has written beautifully of how Gustave Flaubert's fiction represented the moment when equality turned into common sense in late nineteenth-century Europe.[11] Flaubert's most famous and best-loved character, Emma Bovary, was a woman who had the capacity and desire to experience forms of life to which, under previous political and literary regimes, only the elite were entitled. She did not use this capacity particularly well, and the final pages of the novel that grimly describe her suicide by poisoning are hardly an advertisement for human dignity, but Emma Bovary's tragedy was both singular and everywoman's. In *Madame Bovary* Flaubert had created a perceptual world where characters are free enough to simply move through the events of life, so to speak, by right.

Rancière argues that a 'literary community' is not just a community of writers, readers, publishers, and critics: it is a community that identifies with the forms of being human made possible by the arts of writing. Fiction, especially, is one of the means by which equality, dignity, autonomy become common sense. If the modern European novel told one story about equality, the twentieth-century postcolonial novel told a related but different story about freedom from oppression, memory and self-definition. In both cases, Rancière's point remains: the human capacities, perceptions, relationships, and interpretations disclosed by literature exceed the art itself. It starts to matter, then, when words fail to resonate. When, as now, the language of rights turns to ashes on the tongue, when common sense about what counts as a human life seems bereft of new narratives, what is also lost is the sense of a community that is signed up to ideas about equality, justice, and mutual respect.

In this sense, my new colleague might have been forgiven if he had not also pointed out the second part of my title, 'the humanities,' was also at risk of becoming redundant. Teachers of humanities subjects have grown used to hearing that their subjects aren't doing so well over the past ten years. One response is to point out that humanity isn't doing that great just now either and to suggest that these two developments might be related. Elite institutions will always have space for the arts and humanities, and scholars will always find cause to complain that their specialism is not getting the recognition or funding it deserves. But when the kind of mass education that enables the creation of literary communities starts to disappear, defenders of human rights should take note.[12] Educationalists in countries struggling daily with the realities and cross-generational legacies of war, mass displacement, and trauma, such as Palestine and Rwanda, argue strongly (and, given the scant resources available, usually vainly) for arts and humanities to be taught because they understand the intimate connections between imagination, memory, hope and social and political justice. To nurture a love of reading, in the words of the Jordanian molecular scientist and literacy activist Rana Dajani, is more than a nice-to-have or useful tool of social policy: it is also a means of levering 'collective action at local level to create change.'[13] Literary communities, in short, matter to human rights.

Many with more comfortable lives might think they're too fine-now-thanks to need these kinds of insights. We don't need human rights, or even literature really, they perhaps think, because we already have the kind of equality that gives us the right to make a tragedy out of our own lives because, for instance, like Emma Bovary, we're simply bored stupid with the meaningless excess of contemporary living. The modern novel, along with liberalism, capitalism, and mass media, has done its work. That said, of course, the same people retain the right to live their lives carelessly and vacuously whatever the costs to others in the world. As novelist Arundhati Roy put it when she accepted the Sydney Peace Prize in 2004:

> It's a process of attrition. Almost unconsciously, we begin to think of justice for the rich and human rights for the poor. Justice for the corporate world, human rights for its victims. Justice for Americans, human rights for Afghans and Iraqis. Justice for the Indian upper castes, human rights for Dalits and Adivasis (if that). Justice for white Australians, human rights for Aboriginals and immigrants (most times, not even that).[14]

Where ideas about equality and justice, autonomy and dignity are a given for some, others are offered what in effect can hardly be called human rights at all, but is really a watered-down humanitarianism: bare sustenance, minimal dignity, zero self-determination. Small wonder human rights are struggling to make sense today: for some they are meaningless because they are so self-evident; for others they are meaningless because they are self-evidently absent.

*   *   *

But this hasn't meant that people have given up on either human rights or, indeed, thank God, on poetry, fiction and narrative. As Richard McKeon anticipated, although we will always argue about what they have been or should be, the idea that human rights exist in some form persists across time and in different historical periods. This isn't utopianism, and nor is it some fortuitous adaptability of a uniquely good idea. The idea of human rights persists, in the words of the former Secretary General of Amnesty

International, Salil Shetty, because the 'abuse of power against the powerless' persists. At all levels. From the man who smashes his lover's body, to the greedy developers who clad their buildings with combustible material, to the corrupt regimes that backhand investment, to the governments that make lifting a drowning body out of the water a criminal act, to the ludic gamesmanship of the UN Security Council, the powerful screw the powerless. This is the bottom line. 'And this,' Shetty concluded, 'is why we need some rules of the game, why we need human rights.'[15]

Shetty's lecture, given just before he stood down from Amnesty in 2018, was entitled 'Decolonizing Human Rights.' By decolonizing he didn't just mean getting rid of the fatal moral narcissism that tied colonialism and humanitarianism together in the first place, and that still casts its shadow over development policies and aid agencies. Nor was he referring simply to the self-lacerating critical narcissism that sees all human rights struggles through the historical lens of the West's failure to be as good as it imagines it should be, casting even more shade over other fights for justice and equality that we might learn from. What Shetty also meant was that because human rights are always about the struggle against the abuse of power, they have also been, and will always be, inextricably caught up with the work and imagination of decolonization; whether it be resisting the oppression of past and present colonizers, or of the new regimes and dictators that have replaced them, or of multinationals, or of the harvesting of our lives and minds by global tech and AI.

At this point, we can begin to see how the decolonization of human rights and the decolonization of literary studies and the humanities might be part of a common project. Decolonizing literary studies with human rights in mind does not mean valorizing literature because of the way it humanizes other people. If you need to read a book to appreciate that there are other persons on the planet as human as you, in truth your grasp of human rights is probably not that promising to begin with. The literary humanitarianism that encourages sympathy, empathy, and pity for the less fortunate historically belongs to the same humanitarianism that thought that colonialism improved the lives of others, or that modern technological warfare could made more manageable if we simply had some rules about how far we let soldiers and civilians suffer. Amputated limbs? Regrettable but sometimes unavoidable. Lungs filled with noxious gas? No (or maybe?). Agonized and detailed description of your feelings when you stumble across an escaped slave being tortured to death in a hanging cage in South Carolina in the 1780s (the example is from Letter IX of Hector St. John de Crèvecœur's *Letters from an American Farmer*, published in 1782)? Yes. Having the same man utter anything about his condition other than pitiful little bird-like death-squawks? No.

Literary forms, like political forms, come with hierarchies. When a writer or journalist says he is 'giving voice' to a refugee by including her story in his prose, what he is probably doing is casting her in a narrative that re-makes her life in a form he, and his readers, recognize as human because they're familiar with that particular genre of being human. At its best, this kind of writing forces us to reflect on the moral hall of mirrors we enter when we engage seriously with one another's lives. At its worst, it's simply bad writing, a punishment from the gods for thinking that we have the divine authority to be giving or taking away any other mortal's voice. As I suggest in the next chapter, literary sentiment is important to human rights, but not always because it might sometimes make people better at them. As literary theorists have consistently argued, although reading undoubtedly nurtures empathetic feelings, there is disappointingly scant evidence to suggest that feeling warmth and interest in a character in a novel, or even people in general, means that we are more likely to feel generous towards those in the world who might be asking, for example, for a share of some of our economic and political, as well as our apparently plentiful imaginative, resources.[16] 'The empathy model of art can bleed too easily into the relishing of suffering by those who are safe from it,' writes Namwali Serpell in a 2019 essay, 'The Banality of Empathy':

> It's a gateway drug to white saviorism, with its familiar blend of propaganda, pornography, and paternalism. It's an emotional palliative that distracts us from real inequities, on the page and on screen, to say nothing of our actual lives. And it has imposed upon readers and viewers the idea that they can and ought to use art to inhabit others, especially the marginalized.[17]

Or, as James Baldwin observed in 1977: 'People can cry more easily than they can change.'[18] In the history of moral sympathy and capitalism, the correlation of progressive feelings and progressive change is often not quite the causality it first appears. Literary empathy, like real empathy, is a slippery commodity.

Where writing does join cause with righting is in its creativity—its art. The word 'poetics' comes from the Greek *poeisis*, which translates as meaning to put something new into the world.[19] The malleable rules of literature grant us the licence to arrange words, thoughts, images, and plots in constellations that come at the real world, the world of norms, ideologies, policies and politics, at awkward and often obtrusive angles. Writing allows us to dream, and not only to dream, but to disclose hidden connections, injustices, forms of love, ways of being. Literature is not social work, or a bit of human seasoning to make an inhuman world taste a little sweeter. The kind of writing that has always had the best dialogue with human rights punctures moral self-regard with truth. Restless, dissatisfied, refusing the world as it is, the writers who have put new ways of being human into the world rarely call themselves progressive because they know they are dealing with an incomplete and uncertain project, not least because the forms of human cruelty, like literary forms, change through time. These kinds of writers are necessary to human rights, not simply because they urge moral compassion, but because they create imaginative terms by which it is possible to see injustice—not simply to regret it, but to comprehend it.

Thus, Virginia Woolf in 1938, for example (the subject of Chapter Three), who took on Flaubert's project of inventing a prose for the equality of human life in her fiction, pulled apart the liberal consensus of her own class in her polemic *Three Guineas*, a devasting critique of the assumption that the same moral guardians that had given the world patriarchy, colonialism, capitalism, and nationalism were qualified to preach global pacifism. In the same period, two other women, Simone Weil in France and Suzanne Césaire in Martinique, also took creative aim at the shabby humanism they found themselves being asked to defend against fascism. All three grasped a lesson that more recent human rights defenders have had to learn again recently: that grand and abstract concepts of humanity frequently serve the powerful more effectively than the powerless. For these women, only concrete political and historical struggles could produce the new terms for universal justice that the world so badly needed: for Woolf this meant the feminism of the late nineteenth and early twentieth centuries; for Césaire, anti-colonialism, and for Weil, the never-ending struggle between the oppressed and their oppressors that she believed no human rights regime could end.

It matters that these were brilliant writers, not (just) because they gave eloquence to indignation, but because their words made the worlds they lived in appear as intolerable to others as they were to themselves. In Hannah Arendt's terms, we might say they demand political judgment not simply anguished regret. This is a matter of style as well as moral substance. Defamiliarization is the term that literary theorists use to describe how style can make the world strange, following the Russian formalist Viktor Shklovsky's account of how poetic language interferes with the banality of everyday life. When that banality turns atrocity into everyday cliché, poetic language often starts to do its own kind of human rights work. It makes the world of ordinary cruelty re-appear as properly strange, abhorrent, insupportable.

Much of the everyday violence of our times is revealed in the weightlessness of our language. Hannah Arendt referred famously to the 'banality of evil' by which she meant not that the Nazis were innocent, but that the yeasty lightness of modern horror creeps like a fungus into our political institutions, our lives, our words. That is the real atrocity: that we cancel out other people's lives so thoughtlessly, even when we think we're really not doing anything at all, and even, sometimes, when we imagine we're doing good. There is a relationship, Arendt claimed, between the banality of language and the banality of evil. The clichés, platitudes, half-baked metaphors, fact and value-free words that churn through our public discourse are an index of the extent to which we are unable to hear the words of others. This is one of the reasons why it has proved so easy for regimes to pretend that some lives are expendable, superfluous, unimportant. Today's human rights 'crises' are also a catastrophic failure of resonance.

Refugee and migrant, writing between at least three languages, Arendt was one of the first to disclose what the human condition looked like under modern systems of oppression. She invented new genres of political and history writing in order to do so, because, like many who have spent time in detention centres, migrant communities, or in endless queues for paperwork that may or may not see you over the border, she understood the intimacy between the way something is described and what is being described. She understood what it was like to try to survive in somebody else's banality. You cannot destroy political oppression by using the same language of progress, race-theory, theology, and solution-driven thinking as its architects, she thought. To accurately comprehend the reality you are in, you have to be creative.

As for Arendt's generation in the mid-twentieth century, the urgency experienced by many of the powerless today demands—and is producing—new understandings of human rights and concomitantly new literatures, genres, forms, and new literary communities. In the United Kingdom, poetry and poetics have played an increasingly conspicuous role in describing and resist-ing the exclusions of race, class, and citizenship which are now accepted—not, as previously, as regrettable social problems—but as the new norms of social and political policy. Nowhere has this been more evident than in critical-creative responses to the Grenfell Tower fire in West London, that took the lives of 72 people in June 2017 (the subject of Chapter Four). From the first meeting of the local council after the fire, an outpouring of creative elo-quence has challenged the brittle vacuity of the languages of the state, its representatives, and corporate capitalism. The ongoing failures of Grenfell were and are not simply mishaps of governance and protection, errors of judgement, and of human weakness, that can somehow be corrected with a few policy recommendations and some strategic 'sorry saying'. What is morally outrageous about Grenfell is precisely that its outrageousness has not been registered. As with other invariably racist, careless, weightless, systematic acts of dumping of the powerful upon the powerless, the crime is that there appears to be no crime. In this context, to represent a moral and political reality that is invisible to much of the world—which is exactly what the poets, readers, survivors, and activists of Grenfell have been doing—is to do much more than to humanize an inhuman tragedy: it is to expose how the terms of judgment and justice are currently, and devastatingly, inadequate to our current age of impunity.

This relatively new kind of injustice—the cruelty that hides in plain sight and apparently has neither authors nor agents—produces local pain but is truly global in scope. The Iranian-Kurdish writer Behrouz Boochani wrote his book, *No Friend but the Mountains* (2018) whilst imprisoned as a refugee on Manus Island, mainly in WhatsApp messages that he then sent to his collaborator and translator Omid Tofighian. Like Woolf in *Three Guineas*, Suzanne Césaire in her essays and Arendt in *Origins of Totalitarianism*, Boochani creates a new genre of writing in order to give form and meaning to modern experiences of powerlessness. *No Friend* documents what exclusion looks like from the point of view of the excluded. A modern masterpiece that should never have had to be written at all, the book is an indispensable recent addition to the canon of writing that defines humanity by describing the conditions of its extinction. Where others have forged new forms to describe the slow cruelty of colonial settlements, labour and death camps, Boochani gives us the logic of the contemporary refugee and migrant regime as it appears from the inside.

There is a continuity here that we would do well to acknowledge, as I argue in my sixth chapter. Back in the twentieth century, Arendt posed a question that has troubled human rights law ever since: how do we confront a system that has inured itself against culpability? What do we do with forms of oppression that are morally thoughtless by design? To a large extent, today's anguished humanitarian emoting ('have they no feeling?') is the flipside of a brutal reality where political and commercial institutions, often hand-in-hand, have locked themselves tight against accountability ('they have no feeling and they also have lawyers'). We find it easier to cry than to figure out ways of cracking open the walls of plutocratic capitalism. This a strange enough world to live in when you have freedom of movement, but an impossible place to be if you are one of its prisoners. As Primo Levi was one of the first to recognize, oppressing people on an industrial scale means launching an assault on reason as well as on minds and bodies. 'Every prisoner is convinced that they or their group are *the* critical theorist of the systematic foundation, the chief analysts of the system's architecture,' Boochani writes, some seventy years after Levi:

> But the greatest difficulty is that no-one can be held accountable, no-one can be forced up against the wall and questioned, no-one can be interrogated by asking them 'you bastard, what is the philosophy behind these rules and regulations? Why, according to what logic, did you create these rules and regulations? Who are you?[20]

'*Hier ist kein warum*'—'Here there is no why', was Levi's famous description of the reality of Auschwitz-Birkenau in *If this is a Man?*[21]

In an open letter to Fatou Bensouda (Prosecutor at the International Criminal Court), written just after Boochani's escape from Manus Island in November 2019, the human rights lawyer Itamar Mann argued that *No Friend but the Mountains* should be submitted in evidence in a criminal case against the deliberate human degradation, which is now the new normal in border camps, detention centres, and migrant prisons.[22] It is a brilliant suggestion, not only for its evident justice, but because Mann is also asking us to consider what might happen if we really took the relationship between writing and righting seriously. Writing such as Boochani's, Levi's, Woolf's, Césaire's, Weil's, the poets' of Grenfell, and Arendt's, lays out on the table something that law and policy alone cannot. It carves out a space in the world from which we might begin to grasp injustice from its inside, from the position of the powerless. This emphatically is not the same as the anguished testimony of the agentless victim, whose words in any case have historically proven to be easily vacuumed up by the powerful. This is a writing, rather, that goes some way towards challenging Marti Koskenniemi's suggestion that human rights are part of the normative organization of our lives to go a little further. What if they really were? What if we learned to do human rights (again) by following our writers into the darkest places of our history?

CHAPTER TWO

ONCE MORE WITH FEELING

At the Brisbane Writers' Festival, in September 2016, the American-British novelist Lionel Shriver upset many people with a speech in which she stridently affirmed her right, as a writer, to imagine and represent people unlike herself.[1] 'I would argue that any story you can *make* is yours to tell,' she asserted, wearing a sombrero to illustrate the fact that she, as a writer, had the right to try on as many hats as she liked, whoever the hats belonged to originally. Whatever students on campuses and their 'tippy-toe' moral guardians might think, 'we writers have to preserve the right to wear many hats—including sombreros,' she concluded. Pressed to comment on Shriver's provocation, the writer and critic Claudia Rankine responded one month later:

> Getting up and putting on a sombrero and saying, 'I can do what I want. I have the right to do what I want,' to me is missing the point. What would be interesting would be to talk about why is it in the language of rights? Like, white people should have more stuff? ... 'It's my right to take what I want?' Isn't that the history of colonialism? 'It's my right to take resources. It's my right to take land. It's my right to have slaves.'[2]

The point really is not about whether writers can or should write about people unlike themselves. Fiction has always loved the mysteries of otherness, and in truth writers can write about whatever their markets will take.³ The point is about rights. Rankine was giving Shriver a brief history lesson: the intimate links between imaginative rights and property rights, creative licence, and economic and political appropriation, are at least as old as the eighteenth century, and there is nothing trivial about them. If we're going to defend the rights of writers in the names of freedom and justice, as most writers and supporters of human rights would want to do, we need to think about the entwined history of some of these different kinds of rights much more seriously. Feigning iconoclasm in the name of liberty is not going to hack it.

Had Shriver paid more attention to the political history behind the libertarian bogey of cultural appropriation, she might have defended her rights to imagine other lives with another legacy from the eighteenth century that is commonly evoked in defence of creative writing: the more immediately persuasive argument that imaginative sympathy with others is a moral good. This is the tradition that the British novelist Ian McEwan re-asserted shortly after 9/11. 'It is in the nature of empathy to think one's self into the minds of others,' he wrote in *The Guardian*, in a piece meditating, in some detail, on the agonising final minutes of the victims. 'It is hard to be cruel once you permit yourself to enter the mind of your victim. Imagining what it is like to be someone other than yourself is at the core of our humanity. It is the essence of compassion, and it is the beginning of morality.'⁴ McEwan's central point was that whereas 'we' were overcome with imaginative identification, tormented by thoughts of last phone calls, air beneath feet, overwhelming final love, others, namely the terrorists, were guilty of a 'failure of imagination.' As much is no doubt true (although cold-blooded murderers are also well-known for their all-too vivid imaginings of the suffering of others) and McEwan's was a popular and much-quoted intervention at the time. But the confidence with which the novelist described the moral economies of us and others, not to say the others who are us, was jarring even then. What many felt to be overwhelming was the total and violent shattering of the imaginative co-ordinates that had seemed to hold the world in place on the evening of September 10. Nothing seemed less certain than the core of our collective humanity. The years that followed—Afghanistan, the second Iraq War, Bagram airbase, Guantanamo, the Torture Memos, the Chilcot Inquiry— suggest that that confidence in the West's capacity for moral imagination was indeed misplaced. McEwan's claims about the humanizing power of empathetic imagination—so standard in defences of the moral value of literature—are actually no more necessarily sound than Shriver's defence of her 'right' to imagine what she likes. Both creative and moral legacies would appear to have run out of time; and, with them, quite a few assumptions about the relationship between imaginative and human rights are also left wobbling.

I am not, I hope it's clear, saying that imagination, compassion, empathy and connecting with the suffering of others are useless or capricious things in themselves. Twenty years on, when it has become popular for politicians to flaunt just how little they care about anything other than the venal desires of their electoral bases, it would be perverse to call for less empathy. But we do need to acknowledge the historical and political contexts for those feelings. For human rights advocates in the West, the call to feel more is often partly an anguished response to the calculated unwillingness of their governments to do more. More recently, many have also begun to despair at how easily their ambitions to do good are sucked into the imperative to feel good about your own brand.

All that might be politically and morally solid seems to have melted into wrist bands, sing-a-longs, buckets of change, and monthly standing orders. The moral imagination is willing, but the means to tackle the causes of inequality appear weak and inauthentic. Others still have thrown in their lot with human rights altogether, at least as they were understood in the United States and Europe, and are busy imagining new ways to turn the work of being together into something human and enduring. Whilst one human rights imagination seems to have got thinner and thinner, floating free of either purpose or effectiveness, elsewhere the creative desire for equality, freedom, self-determination, dignity, life, has never been stronger.

And amid all this, across the globe, people are still reading and writing, imagining their own lives and those of others' through poems, books, films, TV, social media, drama, and art. Even as educational accountants squeeze down on the margins for the arts and humanities, even as governments shrink-wrap culture to fit their ideological ends, often deeming the arts more palliative than transformative, we continue to imagine our lives together through words. We hold on to the hope that writing might help chart us to another place of moral and political being. This is not entirely foolish. Reading undoubtedly makes us more imaginative. Words, narrative, and story-telling all push the mind both inwards and outwards; our lives, other lives, become possible, plausible, real. Yet what remains as much a puzzle in some parts of the world now as it was in the eighteenth century is how we might get from imagining other people to agreeing to share resources and power with them. If we're going to find new answers to this question, we need to re-think the history of the connections between the moral and the literary imagination a little more critically.

*   *   *

Uncritical idealism about human rights has not helped us address this problem. Human rights have never been just human rights, whatever the noble ambitions of their inventors and proponents, and neither has literature ever simply been the helpmeet of virtue. The historic rights revolutions of the eighteenth century, as Rankine was quietly reminding us, were as much about the transfer of power—meaning land, property, and enslaved people—as they were about lofty ideas of l'humanité. Many of these transfers were good and great things, but it took a lot of dark and violent history before the political and national rights of white propertied male citizens became the universal human rights that, theoretically at least, belong to us all now. Along the way, there was a lot of imagining and re-imagining of what kinds of person might count as human. Human rights did not flutter across the world like butterflies released from monarchical tyranny. They were tightly coveted and ruthlessly preserved by some; tirelessly and endlessly fought for by others. Women, slaves, indigenous people, religious and ethnic minorities, the unpropertied, had to write themselves into the history of human rights, often at the cost their lives as well as their minds. Many are doing so still.

The growth of moral sentiments, as urged by the thinkers of the Enlightenment, was crucial in creating the imaginative contexts in which ideas about liberty could thrive in the eighteenth century, as was the growth of narrative literature in the same period. As Lynn Hunt has argued, it was the soft power of the novel, as much as the violent seizing of privilege, that helped effectively deliver lessons about human equality in the eighteenth century.[5] Books about virtuous suffering, such as Rousseau's *Julie, or the New Heloise* (1761) and Samuel Richardson's *Pamela* (1740) and *Clarissa* (1747) gave vital empathy lessons for a new age of liberty. Soon after, the abolitionist movement would discover that detailed descriptions of the lives, bodies and minds of slaves, such as Olaudah Equiano's bestselling *The Interesting Narrative of the Life of Olaudah Equiano*, first published in Britain in 1789, were also capable of inciting sympathetic passions. By the mid-nineteenth century, classics such as Frederick Douglass's *Narrative Life of Frederick Douglass, An American Slave* in 1845, and Harriet Jacob's *Incident in the Life of a Slave Girl* (1861) had crafted new aesthetic, moral, and political terms for freedom in the form of slave testimony. 'Argument provokes argument, reason is met by sophistry, but narratives of slaves go right to the hearts of men,' declared a Boston newspaper in 1840.[6]

But the road to rights was more jagged than this up-beat history of the rise of sympathetic passions suggests. The route from narrative to the hearts of men might look direct in terms of feelings, but in truth, the byways of literary humanitarianism have always been complex and circuitous. As the eighteenth-century philosopher David Hume pointed out, moral feelings were all the more necessary in a world in which the market had begun to dictate the terms of human relationships. Moral sentiments flourished partly because some parts of the world were learning to prosper by creating new forms of inequality. The more connected by trade and ambition the world got, the more the gaps in wealth and power opened up, and so the more need for generous imaginings about others.

This is why most literary historians tend to qualify their enthusiasm for the virtuous circles that supposedly emanated from the novel. 'The sentimental revolution in literature that dates from the mid-eighteenth century is not just about new kinds and levels of feeling but also about new ways of ordering works and organizing the worlds represented in them' notes James Chandler in his study of sympathy.[7] The ordering of the world, like the complex and shifting levels of narrative hierarchies and perspectives in the novel, cut in several directions at once. Where you figured in the 'great SENSORIUM of the world' (the phrase is from Laurence Sterne's A Sentimental Journey (1768)), depended on your liberty to move through it, watching, spectating and, of course, speculating. The novel was good at putting this newly mobile, thinking-feeling person, with his developing points of view and unique sensibility, into words. Nor was it simply the case that sensibility and humanitarianism made capitalism look better than it frequently was. The market needed the perception of moral responsibility if it was to function without its creatives and speculators simply ripping one another to bits like wolves even before Wall Street began trading in 1792.[8] Moral sympathy was the flipside of the possessive individualism of the new bearers of rights and economic power. It still is.[9]

The novel was also good at stylizing this new sensibility. If one type of book was about the tough lives of people less privileged than their readers—the servant girls and slaves deserving moral compassion—another provided a more explicitly innovative model for the creative life of the new subject of rights. The Enlightenment philosopher Jean-Jacques Rousseau thought that novels made a better case for liberty and equality than philosophy, and instructed that his protégé Émile should read only Daniel Defoe's Robinson

Crusoe (1719). While books in general were suspect as they gave you only the theory of life, fiction, Rousseau thought, made the revolutionary idea of natural rights feel real. 'Let him think he is Robinson himself' he urged.[10] Émile would learn the trick of naturally assuming his role in the world by pretending to be a man in a book.

Nature in the eighteenth century, however, was nature circumscribed: only the newly empowered subjects of the Enlightenment got to make themselves feel like natural white male propertied citizens. In the same novel, Émile would also have discovered the limits to the idea of natural equality. Crusoe becomes his own sovereign-master, 'prince and ruler of my kingdom'—this is the lesson he has for Émile. But it did not follow that rights cascaded down to all in the kingdom. The only 'person permitted' to talk to him, for example, was Poll, his parrot.[11] The word 'person' derives from the *persona* in Greek drama—it is the mask we wear in order to be recognized by the *polis*. In law, corporations can also be persons. In works of eighteenth-century fiction, so too can parrots but not, in this one at least, African slaves, faithful old dogs, chickens or goats, all of whose muteness would also have disqualified them from having a say. The garrulous squawker Poll, of course, being a 'person' as well as a fictional parrot, is male. Man, said Plato apparently, can be defined as a 'featherless biped capable of speech and reason.' Defoe used fiction to bypass the no-feathers requirement. He understood that in an age when being a 'man' accrued you rights to stuff as well as to your humanity, philosophical definitions of man were liable to be politically and legally capricious.[12]

On the one hand, Defoe's novel made possessive individualism seem real and natural. On the other, *Robinson Crusoe* is ironic.

Defoe knows that the fictions he is passing off as real and natural are not quite plausible; he knows that his readers know he is making things up: a male parrot-person named Poll, an immigrant and former slave turned sovereign-master-of-all and role model for future European schoolboys called Crusoe (originally *Kreutznaer*, Robinson's family changed their name so they could assimilate more easily). As the American critic, Wayne Booth, argued, the unstable ironies of fiction beg questions which are deliberately difficult to answer.[13] It all could have been otherwise is also the implication; and so too, perhaps, could have the natural rights tradition.

Lifting the veil on the made-up nature of fiction is a way of questioning the man-made nature of our lives; of asking *but what if things were made up differently?* That is why some claim that the novel form is intrinsically subversive, and thus the foremost most effective literary genre of democratic dissent. But, like its close cousin satire, irony can also cushion the dodgier comforts of knowing resignation. The dead know nothing of our grief, Adam Smith noted in the opening pages of *The Theory of Moral Sentiments* (1759). Or as Rousseau himself famously put it:

> In giving our tears to these fictions, we have satisfied all the rights of humanity without having to give anything more of ourselves; whereas unfortunate people in person would require attention from us, relief, consolation, and work, which would involve us in their pains and would require at least the sacrifice of our indolence.[14]

In the long history of sentimentalism, there's always been a bit of bad faith in the idea that our generous feelings might make a difference to anybody other than ourselves; often that wasn't really the point after all.

In the closing years of the twentieth century, the philosopher Richard Rorty made a version of this sad irony central to his influential account of liberal progressivism at the end of the Cold War. His book *Contingency, Irony and Solidarity* (1989) gave literature and narrative a central role in keeping something like human rights going in a world in which the big narratives about equality appeared to have failed. The virtue of literary narratives, he argued, is that they know that their claims are contingent. Writers, unlike philosophers of history and instrumentalized reason, do not make bad realities—the gulags, camps, censorship—happen. The self-reflective hazardousness of storytelling is its real moral strength. Where reason had clearly failed to persuade people of universal human rights, equality, and liberty, or had persuaded them in ways that led to terrible results, a more modest critical-literary sensibility could at least generate a human solidarity, of sorts, by sensitizing us to other people's pain.

Rorty's version of moral sympathy was essentially a postmodern description of the unhappy Western liberal, reconciled to the loss of big emancipatory narratives, but profoundly troubled by the fact that others were left suffering. We need to keep generating compassion for 'people unlike ourselves,' he urged, but now this endeavour is premised on the ironic recognition that things are unlikely to get much better. Keeping sentiments progressive was the best—or least bad—thing to be hoped for. 'Victims,' he wrote, I assume unironically, 'are suffering too much to put new words together. So the job of putting their situation into language is going to have to be done for them by somebody else. The liberal novelist, poet, or journalist is good at that.'[15] Lionel Shriver and Ian McEwan would no doubt agree. Some people get all the best jobs. The problem here is not only the casual sweeping of the prose of the rest of the world into the private empire of the liberal literary imagination. The problem, again, is also with the idea that the liberal moral imagination is going to automatically give us human rights or even, as in Rorty's minimalist version of rights, a politically useful apprehension of the pain of other people. It is still not clear, if it ever was, that they do, or, indeed, that the version of moral sensibility supported by the imaginative legacies of 'the people of who dreamt up human rights' (as Rorty put it in a lecture for Amnesty in 1992) are the right ones for today—or even yesterday.[16]

* * *

We tend to think about human rights, usually correctly, as progressive, yet things have never really been that straightforward. 'There is no innocent literature,' Jean-Paul Sartre asserted in a lecture he gave for the opening of UNESCO (The United Nations Educational, Scientific and Cultural Organization) at the Sorbonne in 1946.[17] The European novelist faced an impasse in the post-war age of human rights, Sartre argued. On the one hand, the novel is a progressive form. Prose makes injustice visible:

> From the moment in which I give a name to my neighbour's conduct, he knows what he does. In addition, he knows that I know it, and in consequence his attitude towards me is modified. He knows that others know it or could know it, and his conduct comes out of the subjective and becomes part of the objective mind. Literature, therefore, precisely because it is prose and it gives names to objects, consists in moving immediate, unreflected, perhaps ignored actions on the plane of reflection and objectivity.[18]

Fiction names and shames: it makes us reflect on otherwise invisible suffering and injustice. 'The oppression of negroes is nothing',

Sartre offered as an example, 'so long as nobody realises it...but it only needs a word for the act to take on the meaning.' His example was timely. Just one year later, as the United Nations Declaration of Human Rights (UDHR) was being debated, W E B Du Bois and the National Advancement of Colored People (NAACP) petitioned Eleanor Roosevelt, Chair of the Human Rights Commission, to bring the rights of African Americans before the UN. She refused.

Writers are good at representing freedom, Sartre argued, because unlike those in the texts produced by lawyers or policy makers, their words give us pleasure. Reading is an aesthetic experience. As Kant first explained, when we exercise aesthetic judgment, we also enact a kind of freedom by choosing to like, or not to like, what we are experiencing. Novels are brilliant at teasing our judgment, turning us one way and then another, which is why there is a strong truth to the idea that the novel embodies the kind of democratic freedom necessary to human rights cultures. As Kant also pointed out, aesthetic judgments can only happen in political contexts where you actually have the freedom to judge among other people in real life. The anti-communist dissident Czech writer Milan Kundera had something similar in mind when he spoke of the 'sweet lazy liberty' of the novel in a speech he gave as he accepted the Jerusalem Prize for Literature in 1985.[19] Kundera's work was banned in Czechoslovakia until 1989, so he had more reason than many for affirming the pleasures of literary liberty. Novels can sometimes even resist the judgments of their authors, he added, such are the intoxicating powers of free narrative. Tolstoy, for example, set out to write a censorious novel condemning his heroine in *Anna Karenina*, but ended up creating a character he clearly also loved in his own way. For Kundera, as for other writers in the Soviet bloc, the novel was a kind of 'anti-politics'. As Brian Goodman has argued, it was because human rights in the 1970s also played into the idea of being anti-political that the alliance between righting and writing became so strong and, arguably, eventually successful.[20] Both human rights and modern literature thwarted the kitsch bureaucratization of life under totalitarianism and the commodification of human desire under capitalism; both demanded the freedom to judge, enjoy, be wrong, or—in Kundera's delicious example—as Flaubert showed us, just to be stupid in interesting ways.

Back in 1946 Sartre, more sympathetic to anti-colonialism and socialism than the new discourses of humanism and human rights, doubted that the liberties of the European novel would make the post-war world any freer, or any less dangerously, and intolerably, unequal. Whilst it was the responsibility of European writers to defend and promote 'habeas corpus, freedom of thought, [and] political freedom', he insisted they do so with a keen appreciation of the fact that 'at the same time that these principles are no more than a formula of mystification for millions of people.'[21] Unless social, economic, and racial injustices were addressed, human rights would remain the privilege of the few, and large claims about the democratic liberties of novel writing and reading simply, not sweetly, lazy.

Today, Sartre's scepticism would appear to have been borne out. Overclaims for the moral and political value of liberal literary sensibility currently ring hollow. Twenty years ago, Rorty could still write of the rise of 'literary criticism to pre-eminence within the high culture of democracies.'[22] If that was a tenuous claim then, right now it sounds like a statement from another planet. 'Post-critique' is the term some literary theorists are now using to describe the way in which the knowing hermeneutics of the literary ironist now seem out of tune with the times.[23] This might be neither a cause for lament nor a reason for political quietism. At the very least, the demise of comfortable assumptions about literary progressivism brings some of the starker realities—and the starker ironies—of thinking, feeling, and reading in a structurally unequal world back into view. There really is no innocent literature.

And nor are there innocent human rights. The extraordinary moral, political and legal energy that went into the remaking of human rights after the Second World War created the institutions that make it possible for us to discuss, legislate, and argue for human rights today. We tend to assume that this was also a moment when moral sympathy, international law, and a lot of good intentions came together to set up a lasting, working monument to grief that would enshrine the principle of universal humanity at its centre. Because the 'rules of natural law were flouted', argued the philosopher Isaiah Berlin, we 'were forced to become conscious of them' again. Human rights were rebuilt through a shared 'memory of atrocity.'[24] And, to a large extent, this was all pretty much true.[25]

In his influential Tanner Lectures in 2000, from which I also take the Berlin quote above, the writer and academic Michael Ignatieff argued that post-war human rights were essentially a reassertion of the belief in the continuation of moral progress after Auschwitz. Ignatieff opened his first lecture with an unforgettable scene from Primo Levi's *If this is a Man*, in which Levi describes his 'examination' by Dr. Pannwitz, head of the chemical division, who would determine whether he could work in the chemical factory and live (as he indeed did), or die in the corpse factory that was the primary business of Auschwitz-Birkenau:

Pannwitz is tall, thin, blond; he has eyes, hair and nose as all Germans ought to have them, and sits formidably behind a complicated writing-table. I, *Hätfling* 174517, stand in his office, which is a real office, shining, clean and ordered, and I feel that I would leave a dirty stain on whatever I touched.

When he finished writing, he raised his eyes and looked at me...

[T]hat look was not one between two men; and if I had known how completely to explain the nature of that look, which came as if across the glass window of an aquarium between two beings who live in different worlds, I would also have explained the essence of the great insanity of the third Germany.[26]

'He knows that I know it and that others know it or could know it,' as Sartre might have said of Levi's controlled, precise, devastating, description of how the meaning of genocide can be contained within just one look. 'Human rights', Igantieff claimed, 'was a response to Dr. Pannwitz.'[27] Rights were there precisely to empower us to resist the state-sanctioned command of that look, to intervene on behalf of humanity.

Ignatieff's was a powerful ideological reading of Levi, but only partly true historically. Whilst Nazi atrocity and the threat of totalitarianism indeed drove many human rights legislators in the mid-1940s, the Holocaust was kept, at best, to a subtext in this period; it was the monstrous genocide in the room that everyone saw, dimly or all-too-clearly according to their histories, but that was rarely addressed explicitly. There was next to no Jewish witness testimony at the Nuremberg trials. Primo Levi originally struggled to get even a small Italian press to publish his memoir, and it wasn't until the late 1950s that *If this is Man* was translated into English. The trial of Nazi Adolf Eichmann in Jerusalem in 1961 began the process by which the memory of the Holocaust came to furnish late twentieth-century rights with a moral and cultural imaginary.[28] It was that later manifestation of moral imagination that Ignatieff was really appealing to in 2000 as part of a, by then, larger general case for the West to reassert its role as moral custodian of the world after the break-up of the Soviet Union. Ian McEwan's confidence about where the essences of moral imagination began and ended also owed something to this moment.

Ignatieff was on firmer historical ground with his claim that human rights were intended to return the 'European tradition to its natural law heritage'. This was a return designed to 'restore *agency*'—to give us a power beyond nation state and their governments to insist that cruelty stop, that insanity should end. It was also a return that allowed a belief in the progress of moral sentiments to continue, albeit in a more muted form. Levi's essential human rights lesson, Igantieff wrote, was that we can still 'make progress to the degree that we act upon the moral intuition that Dr. Pannwitz was wrong: our species is one, and each of the individuals who compose it is entitled to equal moral consideration.'[29] I'm not so sure that distinguishing our moral and political actions from those of a Nazi who had volunteered to work in Auschwitz signals great progress in moral sensibility. I also suspect that what Ignatieff saw as progress was in reality more of a repetition of the same compromised moral imagination of the natural-rights tradition.

In a story now often told in human rights literary scholarship, when the drafters sat down to debate Article 29 of the Universal Declaration of Human Rights (1948) it was, once more, to *Robinson Crusoe* that they turned to settle the question of what kind of person ought to be the subject of rights. Back in 1948, there was an advance of sorts in terms of thinking about rights and obligations to the communities in which we live, and not only about the right to make and own stuff. In its final form, Article 29.1 reads: 'Everyone has duties to the community in which alone the free and full development of his personality is possible.' The debate, which at times resembled a literary seminar, originally turned on which interpretation of Robinson the drafters could agree that the world now needed: the possessive individualist? The pre-capitalist making only what he needed, as Marx had once argued in his reading of the novel? The Robinson who built a new world out of the wreckage of colonial capitalism? The final compromise gave us a person who was free to develop himself, to wear all the hats, but who was morally bound and attached to the community that gave him those freedoms. As literary theorist Joseph Slaughter first observed, once more the novel form proved itself peculiarly well-suited to expressing how it is we can be made (up) and free at the same time.[30] To say that human rights are a kind of fiction, in this sense, is again to affirm the historical forms of creativity required to put them into the world.

But where the natural rights tradition once owed much to the revolutionary and emancipatory forms of the novel, as Sartre suspected, some of the moral imagining that went with the new age of human rights was going to be as compromised as the old. Demands for decolonization, universal education, and political and economic rights surrounded and nourished the post-war human rights movement. The drafting committee of the UDHR was geographically, ethnically, politically and ideologically diverse. If the document still resonates powerfully now, this is as much because of the political and moral imagination, not to say the tenacity, of progressives from the South, as anything else. Without feminists such as Hansa Mehta from India, for example, and

Bertha Lutz from Brazil, we would have ended up, yet again, with the Human Rights of all Men.[31] That said, nobody in the *Palais de Challiot* in the autumn of 1948 was arguing that Crusoe's Man Friday might also be entitled to rights, duties and a freely-developing personality.[32] Whilst the right to self-determination for all peoples was on the new human rights agenda, it was still marked in fairly faint ink.

It was not until after the 1955 Asian-African Conference in Bandung, Indonesia, that the emergence of the non-aligned movement created the context for the Third World to redefine what human rights might mean in a truly universal context. If the 'memory of European horror', to recall Isaiah Berlin, helped generate the idea of human rights among the powerful, it was through the work of decolonization that they evolved and spread.[33] It was thanks to the arguments of members from Asia, Africa and the Middle East that the oppressions of race and religion found their way into the lexicon of global justice in the United Nations in the latter half of the twentieth-century. The struggle to define historical acts of racial and economic oppression—apartheid South Africa, the Israeli occupation of Palestine, debt-by-design—as crimes against humanity has continued ever since.[34]

Bandung was followed by milestones in the canon of anti-colonial literature and theory: Chinua Achebe's *Things Fall Apart* (1958), Frantz Fanon's *The Wretched of the Earth* (1961), Aimé Césaire's *Discourse on Colonialism* (1972), Alex La Guma's *The Fog of the Season's End* (1972). The modern literary history of human rights begins as much, if not more, with this writing as it does with the ghostly returns and revivals of eighteenth-century legacies of moral imagination in the West. If those latter imaginative legacies now seem enfeebled, and if what we now have is petulant writers in sombreros, this is not because creative writing has lost its power to imagine freedom or produce new genres and forms for human rights. It is because we're still trading human rights on the legacy of a literary tradition that long ago became something of a subplot in emancipatory narratives.

When he collected his own award in Jerusalem two years after Kundera in 1987, the South African writer J M Coetzee gently checked his predecessor's enthusiasm for the freedoms of the novel form. The subversive liberties of the novel are not possible in the conditions created by colonialism, Coetzee argued:

> The deformed and stunted relations between human beings that were created by colonialism and exacerbated under what is loosely called apartheid have their psychic representation in a deformed and stunted inner life. All expressions of that life, no matter how intense, no matter how pierced with exultation or despair suffer from the same stuntedness and deformity.[35]

Deformed and stunted. Coetzee himself would be criticized for assuming that the struggles against apartheid and the legacies of colonialism could only produce a mutilated literature. Was this life itself that was being stunted, or more narrowly, a version of the inner life as imagined by the European novel? What if there were other forms of imagining freedom, other ways of constituting rights in fiction, poetry, and prose? Wasn't he implying there was no African writing?[36] And what is wrong with deformed and stunted anyway? Maybe the distortions of oppression and circumstance also make for unique literature?

Kundera had also opened his own speech with a bizarre and similarly politically maladroit image of literary mutilation. Europe was no longer a body in which the life of the novel could beat.

Israel, he claimed, was now the 'true heart of Europe, a peculiar heart outside the body.'[37] 'Deformed and stunted', a macabre beating-heart pulsing alone. By the 1980s it was as though the tradition of the European novel as a medium for freedom and moral sympathy could survive only in descriptions of its mutilated body parts. Perhaps Kundera could not have known quite how appositely peculiar the idea of Europe's vivisected body beating macabrely on in Israel would have seemed to many by the mid-1980s—or maybe he did and the ironies of his statement are even thicker than they first appear.

In 1986, the year between Kundera accepting his prize in Jerusalem and Coetzee his, the Palestinian poet, Mahmoud Darwish, published his prose poem *A Memory for Forgetfulness*. The text focuses on one day, 8 August, 'Hiroshima Day,' in West Beirut in 1982. The civil war in Lebanon was raging. Under the oppressively violent late summer heat, in a time that seem arrested in repeated atrocity, Darwish's writer-narrator imagines his death with his own striking image of literary mutilation:

> Was it to overcome the ugliness of this fact that the human imagination the inhabitant of the corpse—opened a space to save the spirit from this nothingness?' he asks: 'Is this the solution proposed by religion and poetry? Perhaps. Perhaps.[38]

A torn-out heart still beating. A stunted and deformed body. The human imagination clambering out of its own corpse to save the spirit. Hiroshima, totalitarianism, genocide, apartheid, late colonialism, occupation, war. Put these images and histories together, and what you get is a cut-out collage of the moral and literary imagination in the late twentieth century. If the images refuse to assemble themselves into a singular moral or political narrative, this is because the history they reflect is very far from sorting itself out.

It is tempting to see the return of the enthusiasm for discourses about moral empathy and literary ethics at the end of the twentieth century as an attempt to disavow or at least circumvent some of the difficulties posed by these moral, political, and imaginative mutilations. Joseph Slaughter has recently written of the 'hijacking' of Third World human rights by Western advocates in the 1970s and early 1980s who, whilst nobly determined to protect the individual from the consequences of Dr. Pannwitz's unseeing gaze, could not yet grasp that their way of doing human rights might sometimes be part of the problem.[39] If there is one constant in the history of moral sympathy it is that it seems to increase at the precise point at which moral feeling for others is threatened by an altogether tougher politics; one that might involve the giving up of certain rights—rights to land, power and property to be sure, but also the associated rights to imagine what other people do or do not imagine, or to put their histories into words because you assume they're too dehumanized to do so themselves.

* * *

Does literature give us the moral sympathy necessary for human rights, as is so often claimed? Not really, or at least historically it has done so only by very circuitous routes and then with often messy, complicated, and ambiguous moral and political consequences. But it by no means follows that we are done with the writing and righting project. As the following chapters hope to show, it is because literature can also help us to think and judge in creative and unusual ways, as much as feel in perhaps some rather tired ways, that writing remains vital to the work—not of dispensing human rights to people unlike ourselves—but of creating the political contexts in which it is possible to grant one another what Hannah Arendt first described in 1949 as the 'right to have rights.'[40]

Arendt had little patience with post-war revivals of the natural rights tradition. It was clear, she wrote, that the world had found 'nothing sacred' in the mere fact of being human.[41] As far as she was concerned, the Rights of Man were as dead as Defoe's parrot by 1944. One of the first things Arendt did after the war was reread Kafka. Feeling empathy for Kafka's characters is difficult because, maddeningly, they seem to accede to the power that marks their fate. For Arendt, that dreadful, inevitable living-death feeling is the point. Reading Kafka doesn't generate sympathetic moral sentiments, but something less comfortable. That's also the point, and why Kafka does not offer us an ironic perch from which to sensitively despair at the injustices of the world. In his world, dehumanization is everyone's fate.[42]

Arendt was not alone among mid-century European writers in her impatience with the revival of human rights. 'To contrive a little kingdom, in the midst of the universal muck then shit in it, ah that was me all over.'[43] This was Samuel Beckett's contemporary Robinsonade from his 1946 novella, 'The End', first published in *Les Temps modernes*, the same year as Sartre's UNESCO lecture. A natural rights tradition that had so comprehensively shat in its own backyard was hardly the place to begin rebuilding political morality. Beckett wrote his story after a stint working for the Irish Red Cross in Saint-Lô, Normandy. The city had been laid to waste by the US air force in 1945. From his counting-shed amid the ruins, he found the blithe charity of humanitarianism—the 'having and the not having', as he put it in an un-broadcast radio talk—severely wanting. Like Sartre, he looked at the world dispassionately in 1946 and thought that what was needed was less moral sentiment and more imaginative solidarity. In his broadcast, he spoke of a collective 'smile deriding, the having and the not having, the giving and the taking, sickness and health.'[44] Beckett's weeping, like his laughter, is always shared; that's why it feels so intimate despite all the muck and squalor.

Theodor Adorno once wrote that 'history swallows up existentialism' in Beckett.[45] What he meant, I think, was that the project of being with others that is so intricately, and often hilariously, documented in Beckett's writing always runs into a moment when brute history won't even grant you the freedom to despair. We can call this absurd, and we would be right, but these moments of profound failure are also moments of reality testing: they demand that we must go on—writing, imagining, being-in-the-world—in the full knowledge that massacres and suffering are man-made crimes that we inflict on one another. Moral sentiments, not even when ironically self-conscious about their own inadequacy, will never be enough to make this reality okay. Beckett would have grasped the chastened hope of Darwish's image of the human imagination inhabiting its own corpse immediately. 'Was it to overcome the ugliness of this fact that the human imagination— the inhabitant of the corpse—opened a space to save the spirit from this nothingness?' We can still hope.

CHAPTER THREE

EXPERIMENTAL HUMAN RIGHTS

Virginia Woolf's Three Guineas

...we can best help you prevent war not by repeating your words and following your methods but by finding new words and creating new methods.

Virginia Woolf, Three Guineas[1]

...the temerity of Woolf's version of 'Why War?' does not make her revulsion against war any less conventional in its rhetoric.

Susan Sontag, Regarding the Pain of Others[2]

Susan Sontag was half-right about Virginia Woolf's conventional use of rhetoric in *Three Guineas* (1938). At the heart of Woolf's brilliant, blistering polemic was an obvious truth: war and fascism are the creations of men. This is why she qualifies her support for mainstream peace campaigns on the eve of the Second World War. I will only give you one guinea, she replies to the young man, a lawyer, who had written to her asking for support. *Three Guineas* is a 285-page argument in defence of that reply. Practically her last non-fictional public statement on the state of the world as she found it, the essay is an indictment not only of patriarchy, capitalism, fascism, and militarism, but also of the progressive liberal internationalism of her own milieu and its squandering of opportunity in the first part of the twentieth century. It is a more daring, and perhaps a more contemporary, text than we have come to think.

Woolf opens her argument by establishing a common moral ground between herself and her lawyer letter-writer through a set of atrocity photographs, most likely of the bloody aftermath of the bombing of Madrid by Franco's nationalists in late 1936. This is where Sontag's problem with *Three Guineas* begins. The photographs, including those of children's corpses, were widely distributed at the time, and today are viewed as key case studies in the overlapping histories of modern propaganda, atrocity photography, and humanitarian spectatorship.[3] For Woolf, they are simple, appalling, statements of 'fact': 'Those photographs are not an argument; they are simply a crude statement of fact addressed to the eye.' And it is as crude statements of fact that the photographs bind Woolf and her interlocutor together in shared repulsion and, presumably, so too in a bonded commitment to peace:

> War, you say, is an abomination; a barbarity; war must be stopped; war must be stopped at whatever cost. And we echo your words. War is an abomination; war must be stopped. For now we are looking at the same picture; we are seeing with you the same dead bodies, the same ruined houses.[4]

Echo, repeat, agree is Woolf's strategy here: 'You, Sir, call them "horror and disgust". We also call them horror and disgust.' Writing some sixty-five years later, in the aftermath of another European civil war, this time in the Balkans, Sontag counters that Woolf is being naïve if she believes that the shock of such images can inspire anything other than the most transient and superficial collective opposition to war. The photographs 'are themselves a species of rhetoric. They reiterate. They simplify. They agitate. They create the illusion of consensus,' Sontag protests; Woolf has betrayed her own vision. The audacious premise of *Three Guineas* was that there can be no easy consensus in matters of violence and politics, no innocent gender-neutral 'we' in matters of political morality. Yet here she was, barely into her essay, apparently blindsided by the psychological immediacy of photography. 'No 'we' should be taken for granted when the subject is looking at other people's pain,' Sontag admonishes.[5]

Sontag was right about the treacherous political rhetoric of atrocity photographs, and right too to insist, as she always did, that war and suffering demand the most unflinching of moral gazes. But she underestimates the complexity of Woolf's political and creative endeavour in *Three Guineas*. Woolf returns to the Madrid photographs repeatedly; they punctuate her arguments like open wounds: look, see, remember; this is what we are arguing about, the photograph of 'what might be a man's body, or a woman's; it is so mutilated that it might, on the other hand, be the body of a pig.' But the limit marked by the photographs is not only one of existential shock. Woolf's essay is not just an anti-war and pacifist polemic. It is an examination of the historical causes of fascism; its political economy as well as its misogyny; its roots in colonialism and nationalism; its pervasiveness in Europe and, above all, in England. The photographs are there as much to remind us of our complicity in violence as they are to affirm our collective moral repulsion. Woolf lets her barrister-pacifist share her experience of revulsion, to have his 'we', on condition that he—and her other readers—realize how thoroughly all the things that people of their class and education agree upon 'during dinner without much difficulty...politics and people; war and peace;

barbarism and civilization' are implicated in the bombing of civilians and the tearing open of their houses and bodies.[6]

The 'facts' portrayed by the photographs also turn out be related to other stubborn facts that qualify Woolf's enthusiasm not only for mainstream pacifism, but any progressivism blind to the extent to which the structures of English public life are entangled with power, war, and oppression. She takes no prisoners in this respect. No-one is doing nearly enough to change the politics of inequality, barbarism, and privilege. Thus, her friend petitioning for funds to support a women's college also only gets one guinea because Woolf is still waiting for the 'new college, the cheap college' that will not 'segregate and specialize' for 'honour or profit' but create and democratize knowledge.[7] So you want to support women in the professions, she replies to her third supplicant? What of the connection between accumulation, greed, and the imperial war machine? There's little point in leaning into an abattoir. 'For the evidence of the letter and of the photographs when combined with the facts…seem to throw a certain light, a red light shall we say, upon those same professions.'[8] 'The questions we put to you…is how we can enter the professions and yet remain civilized human beings; human beings, that is, who wish to prevent war?'[9]

How stay human, and how prevent war, in an historically and structurally inhuman social and political structure? This is essentially the question that runs through *Three Guineas*. Woolf's writing is so often praised for its teasing and elusive strategies, its soft ethics and affective power, that we have forgotten quite how politically uncompromising her late vision was. Make a word cloud from the text of *Three Guineas* and it is not her famously sly three dots that dominate the picture, but one big, bold word: FACT.

The 'fact' of the Madrid photographs, then, is not (or at least is not only) a fact that binds appalled humanitarian spectators into a spurious and politically feeble universal revulsion. Rather, it is on a level with the same facts that make establishing a stable, neutral, human position from which to meaningfully protest (let alone prevent) war impossible. For all its *politesse*, in the end *Three Guineas* amounts to a refusal not just to donate wholeheartedly to worthy causes, but to play by the political economy its author has been given to work in: 'The giver has no wish to be 'English' on the same terms that you yourself are 'English,' Woolf concludes her letter to the earnest barrister.[10] Echo, repeat, and dissent. This dissent goes further than conventional pacifism. As much as *Three Guineas* is a denunciation of war and fascism, patriarchy and capitalism, it is also an indictment of the moral and political failure of the progressive liberal internationalism of Woolf's own class. This is what also makes it one of the first and, in retrospect, most significant modernist challenges to what in the years following her death would come to be known as post-war human rights.

*   *   *

It took Woolf seven years to write *Three Guineas,* originally conceived in 1931 as the sequel to her classic feminist tract *A Room of One's Own* (1929). In her scrapbooks and diaries, she gathered documents, newspaper cuttings, notes from biographies, histories, and translations, but the material proved unwieldy. She siphoned off some of her growing archive into the family saga that would become *The Years* (1937), but it was not until a Labour Party Conference in Brighton in 1935 defeated a motion against rearmament that she began to write in furious earnest. For Woolf, the left's growing willingness to go to war illuminated the pervasiveness of the structural violence she firmly associated with patriarchy. This was not a popular view. One of her working titles for the argument that would become *Three Guineas* was 'On Being Despised.' It turned out that the only way to defeat fascist violence was with violence. Sontag was justified in her impatience with the purism of Woolf's pacifism. But the fact that Woolf was wrong about the means should not detract from the critical and political salience or, indeed, the experimental creativity, of her essay now.

By 1935 it was clear that if fascism, xenophobia, and cruelty were rising, this was also because the legal and political globalism of the interwar years had failed badly. The world had looked very different to the left-liberal cosmopolitans of Woolf's milieu at the end of the First World War. Then, war was both a modern techno-logical horror and a problem to be solved by equally modern, rational, innovative, political, and legal instruments. The League of Nations appeared to have ushered in a new, forward-looking form of international politics. The work of Woolf's husband, Leonard Woolf, political theorist, Fabian, and author of *International Government* (1916), had been crucial to the foundation of the League, as had the campaigning of feminist groups with which she was associated, such as the Women's International League for Peace and Freedom (WILPF). By the time Woolf was shaking the photo-graphs from Madrid out of their envelope in 1936, the failure of the League of Nations was painfully self-evident. The catastrophic effects of The Minorities Treaties—one of the first efforts at supra-national legal protection—were everywhere, from the pogroms in the East of Europe, to the crowding of refugees into Vienna and Paris, to the newly acceptable faces of ethno-nationalism and militarism. The progressive liberal internationalism of earlier dec-ades, which had once marched hand-in-hand with the aesthetic and sexual progressivism of the Bloomsbury elite, had felt the ground beneath its feet shift and tremor; by the time *Three Guineas* went to press it felt as though it were about to slip away altogether. Some of us who thought that the case for human rights and liberal progressivism had been won in our own time might recognize the feeling.

When Woolf argued that there is no neutral, collective ground from which war can be condemned, she was not, or at least not simply, being perverse: she was also taking stock of the past twenty years of hope, innovation, compromise and now defeat. There were, of course, as many versions of interwar international-ism as there were views on what the League of Nations was for. But whatever utopian dreams the League inspired, in reality its novelty lay not only in bold cosmopolitan affirmations of a world democracy free of national ties. Its work also helped consolidate political, legal, and cultural ideas about the nation and national-ism within an international alliance.[11] Nationalism did not emerge in opposition to the rootless arrogance of modern cosmopolitan-ism, as narratives about the rise of the right in the 1930s (as now) sometimes tend to suggest. New ideas about the nation and the possibilities of international governance were joined at the hip from the beginning. Ethnic nationalism and internationalism were equally bold reactions against state and legal positivism: both appealed to something more vital, be it race or natural law, than rules-based politics alone; both made creative claims to replace the liberal nationalism of the nineteenth century. Woolf's attack on the politics of easy moral consensus was also an indict-ment of the failure to check the nationalist passion that the League and other international instruments succeeded in making norma-tive in the 1920s. This was partly why liberal internationalism had also failed to make good on its progressive promises for women and the colonized, as well as for European minorities who it had, in effect, help create and then failed to protect (fatally, as it turned out).[12]

The bold new experiments of interwar internationalism with its promises of equality and peace, for many, had ended up with a politics of *plus ça change*—but now with added ethno-nationalism, xenophobia and bloodlust. If she was only prepared to give one guinea to the lawyer-activist for peace, it is because Woolf now understood clearly that working for peace did not, if it ever did, necessarily mean working for the rights of the oppressed. If she would only give her feminist sisters in the worlds of work and education a guinea each, this is because she also knew that to buy into the nation is not necessarily to transform its terms. The daughter of an educated man was unimpressed:

> '"Our country"', she will say, 'throughout the greater part of its history has treated me as a slave; it has denied me education or any share in its possessions. "Our" country still ceases to be mine if I marry a foreigner. "Our" country denies me the means of protecting myself, forces me to pay others a very large sum annually to protect me, and is so little able, even so, to protect me that Air Raid precautions are written on the wall.'

Hence Woolf's now famous, if breathless, universal cry: 'For', the outsider will say, 'in fact, as a woman, I have no country. As a woman I want no country. As a woman my country is the whole world.'[13] These words have since earned their place in many lists of inspirational quotes on global justice and/or by women. Yet to read Woolf as uncritically promoting universal human rights beyond her grave—which is how this quote is very often framed—is again to under-appreciate the creative and political verve of her critique in *Three Guineas*.

Three letters addressed to three imaginary interlocutors; a voice that ducks and dives between registers, personae, times, and tenses; rhythmic, repetitive; dense, despairing: *Three Guineas* may not contain Woolf's most crystalline prose, but its experimental forms speak directly to the urgency of its moment like few others in her oeuvre. It is often argued that Woolf was ahead of the curve when it came to the development of human rights in the second half of the twentieth century. Hers is the writing of a free mind working its way through love, loss, memory, and trauma. In her fiction, goes one argument, we find an ethics of care for a self uniquely mysterious to itself, yet also ethically yoked to the lives of others.[14] Woolf's writing, like Flaubert's before her, helped turn ideas about equality and moral interconnection into common sense.[15] The timing was perfect. October 1929 saw the first publication of both *A Room of One's Own* and the adoption of an early International Declaration of the Rights of Man by the Institute of International Law in New York. 'Lock up your libraries if you like; but there is no gate, no lock, no bolt that you can set upon the freedom of my mind,' Woolf had written in her text. The Institute's Declaration began by stridently re-affirming that previous declarations of rights had 'enacted laws not only for the citizen, but for the human being.'[16] That individual human being—with her free mind and unique personality—would become enshrined in the Universal Declaration of Human Rights (UDHR) some twenty years later.

The 'ahead of the curve' argument is grist to the mill to the idea that literary modernism helped furnish human rights with a transformative ethics that would help bring the new subject of human rights into the world.[17] But the connections between modernism and the development of human rights are a little messier than is sometimes assumed by this progressive model. Woolf was not, as is frequently implied, uniquely creating a literary ethics to supplement the blind-spots of the law. Rather, her writing was already fully part of wider and difficult modernist conversations about rights, persons, freedom, and the possibilities for justice.

The crafting of new legal categories of persons in the mid twentieth century was as boldly creative as anything happening in the arts. And, as with the freedoms of literary and creative modernism, these early versions of human rights were not always quite as cosmopolitan as they might first seem. Whilst a new respect for the self and its choices slowly worked its way into law, creating the legal kernel of what would become human rights, as with liberal internationalism more generally, the identification of the rights of the individual was frequently tied—in complex metaphorical as well as legal ways—to membership of the nation.[18] Like Ezra Pound, Wyndham Lewis and Filippo Tommaso Marinetti, modernist lawyers attempted to harness the 'primitive' energy of nationalism and to reshape it with new—this time legal—forms. The 'subjective choice' and personal freedom that Woolf's writing embodied so powerfully was indeed also one of the bold new principles of international law. But those same new modern individuals, putative bearers of rights and freedoms, as Nathaniel Berman has argued, were also identified pretty much exclusively with their membership of the nation.[19] Modernism was never free of nationalism; in many cases the two fed off one another.

Hannah Arendt would later point out that to become stateless was to become absolutely rightless. No natural law can protect us from being 'merely human'. Hence the paradox that you lost human rights at the precise moment you became only, nakedly, abstractedly, human.[20] Woolf, I think, was similarly sceptical of the idea that human rights would ever be strong enough to trump the rights of men, citizens, and the brute politics of nationalism. Certainly, her emphatic rejection of her letter-writing barrister's terms—'The giver has no wish to be 'English' on the same terms that you yourself are 'English'—was a refusal to have her conscience, and so her freedom of mind, tied to one idea of the nation. Her brilliant counter-move in *Three Guineas* was to re-locate the origins of social justice struggles firmly back in the history of feminist campaigns. Feminism, not universalism, not the League of Nations, not the educated barristers of educated men with their petitions and letters, was the real avant-garde of Woolf's version of human rights by 1938. Before there were human rights, before there were international law and international lawyers, there was the campaign for women's suffrage, for education, for an end to the trade in women and children; for rights and justice, yes, but rights and justice on very different terms from those the pacifist barrister seemed to be offering:

'Our claim was no claim of women's rights only'; '—it is Josephine Butler who speaks—'it was larger and deeper; it was a claim for the rights of all—all men and women—to the respect in their persons of the great principles of Justice and Equality and Liberty.' The words are the same as yours; the claim is the same as yours. The daughters of educated men who were called, to their resentment, 'feminists' were in fact the advance guard of your own movement. They were fighting the same enemy that you are fighting and for the same reasons. They were fighting the tyranny of the patriarchal state as you are fighting the tyranny of the Fascist state...[21]

This is the same rhetorical 'you say'/'we say' repeat-differ-repeat technique Woolf used to create the illusion of consensus with her letter-writer. But the word 'same' in these sentences is also a corrective to easy universalism and appalled consensual horror: the same is actually quite different. Woolf was not so much ahead of the human rights curve as bending it back to return claims about rights and justice to concrete social and historical struggles—to facts.

It was not 'justice, equality, and liberty' in their given senses that the women involved in these struggles wanted, Woolf writes: 'they wanted, like Antigone, not to break the laws, but to find the law.'[22] Antigone, in Sophocles' famous play, defied the laws of Creon, the *polis* and the patriarchy, to give her brother the properly just burial his dignity deserved. Creon punished her by shutting her up 'not in Holloway [prison where the Suffragettes were sent] or in a concentration camp, but in a tomb.'[23] Barely five years after the publication of *Three Guineas*, Jacques Maritain, the Catholic philosopher whose moral conceptions of personhood would form one of the philosophical scaffolds of the Universal Declaration of Human Rights, explicitly claimed Antigone's quest for a higher moral law as a precursor of human rights. Maritain saw Antigone as an ancient bearer of natural law whose ethics were now ready to be realized in a version of human rights that owed less to the eighteenth-century rights' revolutions (looking less appealing after Europe's fascist fall) and more to Christian Hellenism.[24] By contrast, Woolf saw her, like the women activists she cites in Antigone's name, not as laying out new laws with old wisdom, but as pursuing

> endeavours of an experimental kind to discover what are the unwritten laws. That such laws exist and are observed by civilized

people is fairly generally allowed; but it is beginning to be agreed [except by Maritain] that they were not laid down by 'God' who is now very generally held to be a conception, of patriarchal origin, valid only for certain races, at certain stages and times; nor by nature who is now known to vary greatly in her commands and to be largely under control; but have to be discovered afresh by successive generations, largely by their own efforts of reason and imagination.[25]

Largely by their own efforts. If these are human rights, they are experimental, secular, contingent, to be worked out by each historical and political struggle anew, not by international bodies claiming universal rights, but by particular rational and creative efforts. These are not the natural rights of God, patriarchy, nationalism, and colonialism. They are the unwritten laws that we work out on the ground, often in emergency situations: when a brother needs to be buried, a vote won, a child saved from slavery, an antisemitic boycott resisted (the example is Woolf's), an arms trade opposed. There is no universal consensus, no 'we' in the matter of regarding the suffering of others that is not compromised by the inequalities of power: that's the first part of Woolf's message in *Three Guineas*. But there are concrete struggles: there remain 'these very positive photographs—the photographs of dead bodies and ruined houses' that will, each and every time, demand a response.[26]

Unlike some of her contemporaries, such as Jacques Anouilh whose 1944 adaptation of *Antigone* was performed in Paris and was widely understood as an attack on Vichy, and unlike some more recent feminist and political theorists, Woolf was reluctant to bring *Antigone* into debates about justice, rights, and ethics explicitly.[27] Most of her discussion of the play, including the long passage I have just quoted above, remains, appropriately enough, buried in the footnotes to *Three Guineas*. She understood already, perhaps, that any attempt to instrumentalize Antigone's experiments in political justice risked undermining the force of their creative power—or worse.[28] We will never know what Woolf thought the politics of the post-war new order should have looked like: she chose to end her own life in 1941. What we do know is that in 1938 she rejected any invitation to indulge in 'unreal loyalties' even if it would only cost her a few guineas to salve her conscience. Those 'unreal loyalties' included not only those to the nation, but to a liberal and modernist internationalism that had failed in its mission to keep the peace because ultimately it could not recognize its own complicity with political injustice. That, too, is a human rights lesson we are learning again today.

* * *

Woolf and Arendt were not the only women thinkers who viewed human rights with suspicion at this point in their modern history. Nor was Woolf the only experimentalist writer to bend the forms of language to create different arcs for justice and peace. In one of the last texts she wrote before her own death, barely two years after Woolf's, the philosopher and mystic Simone Weil also evoked Antigone to take on what she saw as a gravely mistaken attempt to carve a new kind of natural rights out of the wreckage of fascism and war. Where Woolf located Antigone in a long line of experimental rights activists, Weil cast her as a mystic whose exorbitant claims for justice had absolutely no place in the mortal world of rights and laws. Maritain had misplaced the sacred when he tried to make Antigone the new poster-girl for human rights, she argued. Creon was quite right to say that Antigone's love belonged, with her, only in 'the other world'. 'And truly,' Weil wrote 'this was the right place for her. For the unwritten law which this little girl obeyed had nothing whatsoever in common with rights, or with the natural; it was the same love, extreme and absurd, which led Christ to the Cross.'[29] Antigone's 'extreme and absurd' love, in Weil's view, must be left to hang in the 'middle air' between heaven and earth. By contrast, human rights belong to a political economy of exchange and contest, and so are yoked to histories of imperialism, war, and colonialism. 'To possess a right implies the possibility of making good or bad use of it; therefore rights are alien to good,' Weil wrote. A 'serious politics', by contrast, would begin not with rights, for even to share rights is to acknowledge a world in which inequality is the norm, but with our duties and obligations to one another.[30]

In the period between Woolf's death and Weil's, the writer and anti-colonial activist Suzanne Césaire was writing in *Tropiques*, the celebrated literary modernist magazine published in Martinique, of how supposedly French values, of 'liberty, equality, and solidarity' were part of the 'great camouflage' used to cover up policies of enslavement, colonialism, and racism. Where Woolf had used ventriloquism, repetition, and montage in *Three Guineas* to argue for new experiments in political morality, Césaire drew on surrealism and its 'massive army of negations' to weaponize an alternative language for justice:

> Millions of Black hands, across the raging clouds of world war, will spread terror everywhere. Roused from a long benumbing torpor, this most deprived of all people will rise up, upon plains of ashes.
>
> Our surrealism will then supply them the leaven from their very depths. It will be time finally to transcend the sordid contemporary antinomies: Whites-Blacks, Europeans-Africans, civilized-savage... Colonial idiocies will be purified by the welding arc's blue flame.

The mettle of our metal, our cutting edge of steel, our unique communions—all will be recovered.

• Surrealism, tightrope of our hope.[31]

Where Woolf reached back to the struggles of English feminism, Césaire looked forward to black insurrection 'across the raging clouds of world war.' Both women drew on the creative sources of their art to protest against the failed humanisms they were now, in 1938 and 1943, being asked to defend. Woolf, Weil, and Césaire are very far from the image of women writers granting human rights their imaginative ethical terms *avant la lettre*, by offering a soft touch to hard law, or a kinder sensibility for an atrocious world. They were avant-garde political-moralists refusing those terms and their compromised histories for the sake of something—as yet unrealized—more uncompromising.

At the same moment that Woolf was checking the proofs for *Three Guineas*, Weil was writing her own extraordinary essay on war, peace, and political failure, 'The Power of Words.' Weil, then aged 25, had volunteered in Spain, but had returned home after a scalding accident. She was not at the point—at least not in any straightforward way—a pacifist, but she was a dissenter. In 1937, it was rumoured that Germany had turned its sights on Morocco. Just as in Britain, France had begun to suck on ideas about arming up and protecting its colonies. Weil was as unimpressed with French jingoism as Woolf had been with the Labour Party's endorsement of re-armament in the same year.

There will always be struggles, she argued: the privileged will always try and protect and justify their lot, and the oppressed will always fight back. But the war the world was heading for, she warned, was essentially over words that had been emptied of meaning. Grasp a word such as 'national', she wrote 'all swollen with blood and tears, and squeeze it, we find it empty': empty save 'millions of corpses, and orphans, and disabled men, and tears and despair.'[32] The camouflage had been revealed for the thin, mottled disguise it was. What was left was violence without meaning. No less than Woolf, Weil understood that in an unequal world, peace and privilege are uneasy bedfellows. With a clarity that still startles, she concluded her essay with a passage that could act as a coda for *Three Guineas*:

> There are no more dangerous enemies of international and social peace than those spell-binders whose talk about peace between nations means simply an indefinite prolongation of the status quo for the exclusive advantage of the French State or whose advocacy of social peace presupposes the safeguarding of privilege, or at least the right of the privileged to veto any change they dislike. The relations between social forces are essentially variable, and the underprivileged will always seek to alter them; it is wrong to enforce an artificial stabilization. What is required is discrimination between the imaginary and the real, so as to diminish the risks of war, without interfering with the struggle between forces which, according to Heraclitus is the condition of life itself.[33]

'War, you say, is an abomination; a barbarity; war must be stopped; war must be stopped at whatever cost', Virginia Woolf wrote to her earnest young barrister. 'And we echo your words. War is an abomination; war must be stopped.' But although they were looking at the same picture, seeing the same dead bodies, the same ruined houses as Woolf, like Césaire and Weil from their very different outsider societies understood, they could not be on the same page so long as privilege was uncontested.

CHAPTER FOUR

WORDS OF FIRE

Creative Citizenship

O n 19 July 2017, one month after the Grenfell Tower fire, the Royal Borough of Kensington and Chelsea Council held its first meeting.* The public gallery was packed to capacity. People, including residents of the Tower, friends and relatives of the dead and injured, queued outside. The elected officials sat on their benches, individual chilled bottles of water before them. After the Mayor's Special Announcements, and before debate turned to matters concerning the appointment and duties of the electoral returns officer, those who had been 'involved in the Grenfell Fire Tragedy' were invited to 'come forward and speak'. What followed was an outpouring of fiercely eloquent grief and rage.

It was an extraordinary meeting but not, as some of the British press chose to report it the next day, because the business of

---

* On the night of 14 June 2017, a social housing tower block in West London caught fire. By morning, seventy-two people had lost their lives. The people who lived in Grenfell Tower had warned their local council repeatedly that recent refurbishments to the building had rendered it unsafe. The British government set up an Independent Inquiry in September 2017. Phase One of the Inquiry, on what happened that night, reported in October 2019. Phase Two, on the causes and circumstances of the fire, is on-going at the time of writing.

democratic governance was interrupted by the unruly passion of residents and activists. The passion spoken in the council chamber *was* democracy—as many of those present, and those (like me) who were watching the live-stream of the meeting, could see clearly. In this chapter, I return to that evening to argue for the power of creative citizenship. More straightforwardly, I also want to help document an event that—as with many chapters in the history of Grenfell—otherwise risks being consigned to the same archives of forgetting and banalization, racism, and inequality that created the conditions for the tragedy in the first place.

Many people claimed their human dignity back in the Council Chamber, but few did so with such devastating precision as Mahbubeh Jamal Vatan, who took her seat by the microphone, laid her crutch to one side, and began her testimony with these words, spoken in Persian:

I am Mahbubeh Jamal Vatan.

I lived with my son and daughter in Grenfell, no.10

I'm Iranian and begin my speech with a poem by Saʻdi', the renowned Iranian poet:

'Human beings are members of a body/In creation of one essence. /If one member is afflicted with pain/Other members will not remain in comfort.

You who are indifferent to other's suffering/you are not worthy of being called a man.'[1]

Vatan was quoting Saadi, the 'nightingale of Shiraz', and his celebrated lines on collective suffering from the classic text *The Golestan (The Rose Garden)* written in 1258 CE. 'You who are indifferent

to other's suffering/you are not worthy of being called a man' are
the last lines of the famous verse with which he closes the tenth
tale from the first chapter, 'The Manner of Kings.' 'You who are
mindless of others' pain/Do not deserve to be called human' reads
a more forceful translation.[2]

Saadi's evocation of humanity has some currency in the cor-
ridors and chambers of global political power. You can find the
same words woven into a carpet that hangs on the wall of the
United Nations Building in New York, a gift to the world from
Iran in 2005. President Obama, or someone in his office, liked
the *Golestan* verse so much that he quoted Saadi as part of
his olive branch new year message to the people of Iran in 2009
the warmest message to Iran from the US to that date, and
certainly since.

As Vatan spoke Saadi's words through her translator, the
Council room fell, briefly, silent. Yet, for all its poignancy, this
was not a moment when poetry made universal humanity happen where it had been (and some would say, remains) absent.
Vatan was doing something much more critically-creative than
simply offering her listeners the comfort of affirming a common
humanity. The lines from Saadi were a direct reproach: 'You who
are mindless of others suffering...do not deserve to be called
human.' Feel our presence, Saadi's lines were also saying. Mind
our suffering. Neither was this a plea from the powerless to the
power-rich. By quoting the poem, speaking its lines, insisting on
being heard—insisting on being there—Vatan was not asking for
but *claiming* her rights to human recognition. Quietly, firmly, and
without many present even noticing, she was enacting her right
to have rights.

It matters, I think, that it was a poem that was spoken in the chamber. Stitched-up and hung-up in the United Nations Building, Saadi's lines struggle to resonate, or perhaps, resonate only as pathos. By contrast, in the stuffy, overheated council chamber that evening, his words were given the opportunity to mean again. On Vatan's lips, spoken in Persian, through a translation to the many different kinds of English spoken in the room, they evoked another kind of universalism. 'We know ourselves as part and as crowd, in an unknown that does not terrify,' wrote the philosopher and poet Édouard Glissant in *The Poetics of Relation*: 'We cry our cry of poetry. Our boats are open, and we sail them for everyone.'[3] It was a similar 'cry of poetry' Vatan evoked with her speech act that was, at the same time, a poetic act and a political act. 'Where is humanity and conscience then?' she concluded her testimony, just in case anyone had missed the point about the emptiness of rights talk implicit in her quotation. 'The human rights which the UK fights for overseas should be respected for the people who live in this country. Why aren't human rights respected here?' Why isn't the language of justice and rights doing more? Why are its words failing?

* * *

'Why aren't human rights respected here?' This is a question that poetry sometimes is better placed to answer than policy. As with many collective tragedies, Grenfell has produced conspicuous amounts of poetry. But in the days following the fire, it quickly became apparent that this human suffering was not available for easy universalizing or memorializing. The inequalities of power and voice, privilege and life, race and class, were too stark and too real to make appeals to universal sorrow sound anything other than, at best, cloth-eared and inadequate. This was not everybody's grief for the taking. Indeed, the question of who 'everybody' was is precisely what revealed itself to be at issue. The Grenfell fire was not only a human-rights disaster, a man-made catastrophe occasioned by policies of austerity and greed. It was a catastrophe in the meanings of democratic citizenship in Britain.

Ten days after the fire, Ben Okri read his poem, 'Grenfell Tower, June 2017,' on Channel Four News. The poem was not only a lament. It was an injunction to respond. *'If you want to see how the poor die, come see Grenfell Tower'* goes the poem's refrain:

> *Those who were living now are dead*
> *Those who were breathing are from the living earth fled.*
> *If you want to see how the poor die, come see Grenfell Tower.*
> *See the tower, and let a world-changing dream flower.*[4]

This is how the poor die; this is what you should *want* to see; not just a tragedy, but an atrocity crafted by the exclusions of wealth, race, and privilege. In the autumn of 2017, Okri hit back at these exclusions in a talk that affirmed the historical power of citizenship. 'A citizen is a living unit of democracy, a living force for the possibilities of this world,' he argued. Citizenship is what 'constitutes a human being with rights in this world.'[5] We are citizens, in other words, or human rights are nothing—which is why pleas for justice for the dead are also claims for the rights of the living. Half-way through his poem, Okri quietly changes two words in his refrain. 'Those who were living now are dead/Those who were breathing are from the living earth fled' becomes 'Those who are living now are dead/Those who are breathing are from the living earth fled.' The 'Ghosts of Grenfell' are not only of the dead, but of the living who, denied citizenship, are also being denied the right to be human, to be seen.[6] To be 'from the living earth fled' is the fate of all those offered only cut-price citizenship.[7]

The Grenfell fire happened almost a year to the day after the UK had voted to leave the European Union. As the power of citizenship exploded into political life, so too did the extent to which that same citizenship had been compromised become clear. Even as the officials of Kensington and Chelsea were snipping at their budgets and light-touching building regulations, the UK's Home Office was setting in place the Hostile Environment policies that would later see people of the Windrush generation manhandled onto planes away from their homes and families, or dying for want of the NHS care they had spent their working lives paying for. The 'first thing that is done in any colonial or imperial enterprise is to redefine the idea of the citizen': up (for the colonizers), down (for colonial subjects), Okri argued in his talk. 'Grenfell Tower did not happen on the day the tower caught fire,' he concluded, 'but in the days and the years before.'

To claim—or reclaim—citizenship in this context could hardly mean accepting the morally and politically repellent terms upon which it is currently understood or grudgingly offered. But it can mean practising citizenship, demonstrating mutual obligation, even as the political terms of belonging are denied. In the hours, days, and months following the fire, the people of the Lancaster Gate Estate came together to give care, shelter, food, and support in a much commented upon upsurge of citizen-citizen humanitarianism. The fire took place during in Ramadan. Itfar baskets rapidly passed between streets, families, and communities. Solidarity has been replayed ever since on the fourteenth of every month, when the people of the Lancaster Gate Estate, with their supporters, march silently through the streets. 'Of all the qualities, the one I most value in the citizen' Okri noted in his talk, 'is awareness':

> Everything else can be bought or smothered or diverted or confused, but awareness asks questions of the world. There are many with excellent education who see the conditions of the world but then rationalise them. Awareness sees them as they are. Then they ask questions. They ask why. Sometimes they ask why not.

A 'living force', a 'world-changing dream,' to echo Okri's poem, a collective silence punctuated only by footsteps and passing traffic: awareness, absence, ghosts. It is not only the abuse of human rights that is the on-going scandal of Grenfell, it is that other necessary and dissenting forms of citizenship are denied political recognition. This might be why poetry has come to matter so conspicuously in the aftermath of the fire: something else needs to be—is being—created.

The poetics of Grenfell—and I also mean poetics here in the active sense of putting something into the world that Marx evoked when he wrote of the poetry of the future—refuses to perform traumatized victimhood in exchange for legal or political recognition.[8] In place of the ethical evocations of memory and empathy that have come to dominate discussion of human rights and literature, writers, activists, and survivors have consistently put the politics of citizenship—and an awareness about that citizenship—back into action. 'They ask why. Sometimes they ask why not.' They also ask, as did Mahbubeh Jamal Vatan on the evening of 19 July, 'why aren't human rights respected here?'

Very little of this kind of creative citizenship is being recorded or archived in the public domain. The silencing of citizens and survivors has become part of the on-going political story of

Grenfell. The livestream video of that first Council Chamber meeting which I first watched in July 2017 is now finally available on the website of the Royal Borough of Kensington and Chelsea Council. The story recorded on that film and, crucially, in the words recorded by the film—tellingly, none of the testimonies that evening were recorded on the official minutes—disclose a different kind of human rights story from the narrative that says Grenfell is a matter of pity, regret, and lessons to be learned by the powerful in their dealings with those less fortunate themselves. 'By simultaneously demanding equality and liberty we reiterate the enunciation that is at the root of modern universal citizenship', writes the political philosopher Étienne Balibar.[9] That, I would argue, was what was happening that evening. By—scandalously according to many of the mainstream media and to the evident discomfort of some councillors—taking the liberty to demand equality of citizenship, the survivors who spoke in the Chamber also re-iterated the rights claims of modern universal citizenship. Universal here should be understood concretely, not abstractly. The dead of Grenfell were British, Irish, Italian, Lebanese, Syrian, Iranian, Indian. They came from Afghanistan, Bangladesh and the Philippines; from Morocco, Sudan, Egypt, Eritrea, Ethiopia, Dominica, The Gambia, and Sierra Leone. Those who spoke in their name were evoking the power of a citizenship not as exclusion, as narrowly understood by the purveyors of the new ethnonationalism in the UK, as elsewhere, but precisely as (to quote Okri again) 'a living force for the possibilities of this world'.

* * *

At least as striking as the poetic eloquence of Mahbubeh Jamal Vatan on the evening of 19 July, was the inability of the words of others to connect to the context in which they were being spoken. Words fluttered both too high and too low; they were at once too many and too few. The newly elected Leader of the Council, Elizabeth Campbell, uttered the words 'I understand' so often that, as when you write your name over and over on a school exercise book, they started to seem meaningless. In truth, there was little understanding in the Arendtian sense of thinking with the words of others in evidence. 'They're listening, but they're not hearing' one participant shouted from the gallery. She had to shout because, like other survivors and activists, she did not have access to a microphone. 'They say "we understand you" but this is not the truth,' as Mahbubeh Jamal Vatan put it in her testimony. Listening without hearing, understanding without moral responsibility, voices without microphones. Even when responsibility was acknowledged, it was hard to escape the impression that many speaking for the Council floundered for want of a credible script. 'I believe in life sometimes you need to step up', attempted the deputy leader, Kim Taylor- Smith, from somewhere within a nineteenth-century feuilleton, 'and I believe for me...' before crashing into cliché—'these poor people'.

Arendt observed that when language fails to resonate, when it starts parroting itself, lifting free from moral context, we are in the presence of what she called the banality of evil: a thoughtless-ness that strips words and actions of their poignancy because it is also, in her analysis, when language disconnects that the everyday business of public administration and governance turns malign and, sometimes, even murderous.[10] 'A man speaks over his action, with a narrative arc that makes everything OK, if incredibly sad,' Grenfell activist Daniel Renwick has written in a searing essay called 'Organising on Mute'. The 'country keeps calm and carries on.' There is something 'evil', he comments, in this process.'[11] The point here is not about evil intent, but the opposite. If more people actually thought about what they were doing or saying, Arendt argued, probably there would be less evil in the world. Cruelty is frequently careless, which is not the same as saying it is excusable.

The apparent insouciance of the words of some officials that evening fluttered close enough to the dark to reveal just how seriously awry the administration of political morality had gone in the Council. 'OK. Thank you very much everyone for your contributions and for telling us your stories, and we will now carry on with the ordinary business of the meeting' concluded Mayor Marie-Therese Rossi crisply, after no fewer than fifteen people had spoken of their grief, terror, rage, incomprehension, and fear, over an achingly long two-hour period. We cannot know whether the Mayor really thought that citizens 'telling their stories' was an activity somehow separate from the work the work of representative democracy that is supposed to go on in council chambers. But the slip, assuming it was a slip, betrayed the extent to which for some present that evening, those telling the stories were more a category of humanity to be managed and administered to ('those poor people') than fellow citizens to whom they were accountable. To 'allow' people to tell their stories was somehow interpreted as doing enough to at least be seen to be acknowledging their rights. The councillors were hardly alone in the assumption that story telling in itself performs a weird kind of human rights magic where nothing much more than listening is necessary for justice to happen—the idea is now mainstream. Not much budged that assumption in the months that followed. In her 2018 report on Grenfell, the United Nations rapporteur on housing, Leilani Fahra, observed that residents were being treated 'less as people with human rights, and more as objects of charity.' 'Residents told me they feel the government's position is that they should feel lucky that they are going to be rehoused and that they should feel lucky that they had social housing,' she wrote; there was little to suggest that 'the government recognises them as rights holders.'[12]

Even as the walls of the UN were being built over 70 years ago, Arendt, among others, predicted that the more the world globalized, the more people were pushed into what she called the 'dark background of difference', the more the abstractions of universal human rights would struggle to grant access to the equality, freedom, and self-determination that would allow people to truly protect themselves, their homes, and their families. Only an active, participatory claiming of the 'right to have rights'—to appear, act, and speak—within a political community of citizens, she argued, could guarantee the mutual recognition of humanity necessary for equal rights.[13] Writing as a stateless person, a Jew, and a refugee, Arendt had the exclusions of the twentieth-century European nation state in mind. Depriving people of citizenship, she argued, was the first step towards making them rightless. Today those exclusions are also internal to states—the 'we refugees' that Arendt wrote of in her essay of that title in 1943 are now groups of workers, migrants, and refugees, living inside the nation, corralled behind glass walls (and flammable cladding) built to defend not just white privilege, but the occupation of public spaces by the private capital that now helps funds it.[14]

When the people of North Kensington began to speak that evening, the glass of one of those walls started to splinter, if just for a moment. Read the Council minutes and next to nothing of this moment remains: 'the council heard a number of very personal and moving accounts of their experiences in this tragedy…' they document, inadequately.[15] Listen to the words that were actually spoken that evening, however, and what you hear is an utterly extraordinary, to my mind at least, collective reclamation of the rights to be seen, heard, to object, to exist. Some examples:

> What part of my body do you want me to give to demonstrate the effort of provoking the humanity in you?
>
> People don't like to be addressed as poor…the people who are poor who are using us for gain…empty people.
>
> If you believe you have the legitimacy…the wounds of North Kensington are not going to heal as long as you are so ignorant to believe that you have the right to rule over us…
>
> You guys rolling your eyes.
>
> Innocent children went to bed and woke up in ashes.
>
> The dead do not want you. We do not want you.
>
> You all have nice fancy bottles of water, we had a jug of water that we had to ask for…a few polystyrene cups…
>
> If you can't respect the dead, how can we believe you are going respect the survivors?
>
> What happened to government? What happened to the history of England? What happened to all the hard work the people before and before you and before you and before you did, and did, over and over again…
>
> I'm burnt up…

The utterances of survivors transformed the context in which they were spoken. Statements started to mean more than their speakers intended them to say. 'You cannot lock the fire escape!' cried one man. 'It's not locked,' replied the Mayor, wearily: 'It's an exit, not an entrance.' As pithy a metaphor as any for a situation in which some people whilst not constitutionally locked out of citizenship, are nonetheless encouraged to exit rather than enter the public realm. Words doubled over, became heated, glowed, and, as they did, the void that stretched beneath the 'ordinary business' of local representative democracy came into view. 'You couldn't make this up' despaired another resident. But they had, and that was also the point. They had made it up, and now another kind of language would have to unmake it.

Words are actions. Poetic words are intense actions, which usually do very little in the world but just occasionally are good at telling us what other languages are failing to do. In linguistics, the 'poetic function' of language is said to be at work when words conspicuously refer to themselves, thickening the air with ambiguity, lifting free of direct reference to context. Such ambiguity, Paul Ricœur argued, does not necessarily suppress reference: it can also alter our relationship to reality.[16] If the banality of our current political language lifts free from any shared sense of reality, a poetics of citizenship is perhaps one way of helping ground it back or, at the very least, as the citizens of the Lancaster Gate Estate showed that evening and since, of enacting injustices so that they can be heard and felt for what they are.

There can be no universal humanity, and no human rights, if people do not have the political rights to make them happen. That was why the testimonies given in the Council Chamber that night were so important. They were human rights claims made in the public realm; statements of citizenship that insisted on being spoken. Being deprived of political citizenship, denied representation or a hearing (let alone chairs to sit on or water to drink on a hot evening), is non-trivial. To be cut out of decision-making, ignored, locked out of spaces of public debate is an attack on human rights because by those exclusions people are being denied the first right, which is the right to have a say in what counts as a human right among the people you live with. And, along with millions of people in the world, those in the public gallery in the Royal Borough of Kensington and Chelsea that evening understood all too well that being granted only non-priority citizenship is not simply a matter of political representation, but frequently of survival itself.

* * *

Balibar has written of the need for what he calls an 'intensive universality' which would give up the all-encompassing territorial ambitions of liberal internationalism, to instead work for 'new interpretations of the principles of citizenship' through collective local and transnational action.[17] Poetry and poetics are good at intensifying universality, as Mahbubeh Jamal Vatan understood when she recited Saadi in the Chamber that evening. This is another reason, perhaps, why literature really matters to human rights: not because it humanizes the inhuman, but because it collectivizes humanity in complicated, and often uncompromising, terms.

Each of the stories in *The Golestan* ends with a classic four-line ornate verse. The verse Vatan cited comes from the tenth chapter of *The Golestan*, and is known as the *bani adam*, the children of Adam:

> When the calamity of time afflicts one limb
> The other limbs cannot remain at rest.
> If thou hast not sympathy for the troubles of others
> Thou art unworthy to be called by the name of a man.

The lines conclude the story of the sage's meeting with a notoriously unjust king whom he encounters in Yahia's tomb in the grand mosque of Damascus. As the corrupt king enters the mosque, the poet notes:

> The dervish and the plutocrat are slaves on the floor of this threshold.
> And those who are wealthiest are the most needy.[18]

'The wealthiest are the most needy.' Or as one of the survivors put it that evening in a contemporary interpretation of the same point: 'People don't like being addressed as poor…the people who are poor who are using us for gain…empty people.'

There are few places on earth capable of producing the kind of radical equality that Saadi advocates. A council chamber in the richest borough in the United Kingdom, one of the richest countries in the world, is possibly about as different from a mosque in Damascus in a classic piece of literature as you can get. But by quoting Saadi's poem to ask, at least, 'Where is the equality? 'Why aren't human rights respected here?' Vatan put the questions of universal justice and equality back into the room. She seized her liberty to speak and in so doing also insisted that Saadi's words be allowed to re-shape what was passing for reality in the council chamber. The enactment of citizenship and the demand for equal human rights didn't make either any more real or likely—otherwise we would be looking at an entirely different political response to the Grenfell tragedy than the one we have now. But it was significant, if only because what Vatan demonstrated so powerfully was the absence of universal citizenship in the Chamber.

Historically, Saadi had an important role in shaping the West's concepts of universal humanity, so we can also think of Vatan citing him in order to bring his message home. Voltaire took his name for his orientalist novel *Zadig, ou la destinée* (1749). Johann Wolfgang von Goethe wove strands of Saadi's life and work into *The West-East Divan* (1819). Johann Gottfried von Herder described him as a 'pleasant teacher of morals.'[19] Ralph Waldo Emerson addressed a poem to him in 1842 and provided the preface for Francis Gladwin's 1808 translation of *The Golestan*. Henry David Thoreau liked Saadi enough to cite him in *Walden* and write about him in his *Journal* (under the telling heading 'Assimilating Saadi'). The eighteenth-century linguist and philologist, William Jones used *The Golestan* to teach Persian, which was how the text also ended up as a primer for colonial administrators at the infamous Fort William College in Calcutta. Saadi may have been nearer to the mindset of some the councillors in the chamber than they knew.

In a final poignant moment that evening, Vatan's translator helped interpret the meaning of Saadi's lines for those in the room more familiar with the English canon of poetry. The meaning of the verse, she explained, is similar to John Donne's 'therefore never send to know for whom the bell tolls; it tolls for thee,' from the famous seventeenth of his *Devotions Upon Emergent Occasions*. Donne had written the devotions when he was sick, feverishly anticipating his own death, and recognizing that thinking yourself better than others does not excuse you from mortality. Individualism, for all that it enshrined the rights of English men in the seventeenth century—and for all the spoken lyricism of Donne's poetry expressed that triumph—came with a price. There is an equality above man; that's what death tolled for Donne, and this is what we are telling you now, the translator gently explained to the Chamber. It was perhaps no coincidence that the other famous lines from the same poem had burst back into the public realm in the wake of the Brexit referendum one year earlier:

> No Man is an *Island*, entire of itself; every man is a piece of the *Continent*, a part of the *main*; if a *Clod* be washed away by the *Sea*, *Europe* is the less, as well as if a *Promontory* were, as well as if a *Manor* of thy *friends*, or of *thine own* were; Any Man's *death* diminishes *me*, because I am involved in *Mankind*.[20]

Running Donne and Saadi together in other contexts might well have produced platitudes in the place of either poetry or politics. But spoken together that evening, alongside the words of citizens and survivors, they did not. They were words of universal intensity. They were words of fire.

CHAPTER FIVE

THE BEWILDERMENT
OF EVERYDAY VIOLENCE

Shamima Begum, Freud, Citizenship and Law

Every television channel replayed it, endlessly…

Kamila Shamsie, *Home Fire*[1]

In February 2019 the UK Home Office wrote to the parents of Shamima Begum revoking her British citizenship. Begum had left Britain to join ISIS in 2015, and now wished to return to her family with her infant son. Days later, a shooting range used the face of the teenager as a target. It was posted on Twitter, captioned with the words 'traitors,' 'made your choice' and 'no remorse.' 'The targets provide some fantastic reactions and conversations and allow people to have some light-hearted fun and bring out the inner child in us all,' a spokesperson for the range said.[2]

There are many different moral and political types of violence going on at once in this unedifying story: the violence of totalitarian terror, the violence of fanaticism, the violence of law, the violence of vengeance, the violence of spectacle and the violence of fantasy ('light-hearted' violence) are all at play. Our first instinct is to discriminate between these violations of life and liberty.

But whereas some forms of violence can of course be judged as worse than others, it is also true that the everyday pervasiveness of these extreme physical and emotional reactions and responses is often bewildering both for those who experience it (willingly or not) and for those who try to study and understand it. This short chapter attempts to untangle some of that bewilderment by thinking about psychoanalysis, law, and fiction.

Bewildering was also how the psychoanalyst Sigmund Freud experienced the shocking violence of the First World War. Freud has had an undeserved bad press in studies of violence, largely because he was often assumed to be talking only about innate and primitive violence, and not its political, social, and historical forms. In fact, Freud himself was always clear that it was as much how violence was imagined, consciously and unconsciously, as brute instinct that was kept in balance by 'civilization'. Wartime, he discovered, was not so much (or at least not only) a letting loose of primal aggression as a catastrophic collapse of the planes of perception that protect the illusion that the citizens of Europe lived in non-violent, 'civilized', and cohesive national cultures. Violence, in short, changes the way we see the world at an extremely intimate level. His essay 'Thoughts for the Times on War and Death', written on the Austrian home front in 1915, opens with this memorable description of the shattering of that comfortable image:

> In the confusion of wartime in which we are caught up, relying as we must on one-sided information, standing too close to the great changes that have already taken place or are beginning to, and without a glimmering of the future that is being shaped, we ourselves are at a loss as to the significance of the impressions which bear down upon us and as to the value of the judgements which we form.[3]

Wartime is not only dead and wounded bodies. To be at war, even as non-combatant, is also to be lost in a whirlwind of images attached to feelings: dangerous feelings, which require targets. There is something violent, Freud was saying, about the perceptual field of conflict itself: its images, the things it does to time, to judgment, to the psyche and to our ability to take our moral and cognitive moorings when impressions are bearing down upon us. Freud was disturbed but not surprised by this everyday violence happening far from the front. Even in peacetime we are always a mess of conflicting drives, in his view; always secretly happy with images of somebody else doing the dying and suffering instead of us, taking surreptitious pleasure in spectacles of human pain; hence the usually culturally benign, and often psychologically helpful, power of drama, art, and narrative. But in wartime these images break out of their frames and that inner violence reveals itself as part of the politics of the everyday.

Freud next says something striking. It is not so much that this violence threatens the state as that it wants it for itself. Like other modern thinkers, Freud thought that violence was structural to democratic governance. 'People are more or less represented by the states which they form, and these states by the governments which rule them,' he writes. But in wartime it became clear that the state prohibits the violence of its citizens 'not because it desires to abolish it, but because it wants to monopolize it, like salt and tobacco.'[4] Violence, Hannah Arendt argued famously, is what happens when politics collapses.[5] It is a failure of politics. From the generation before her, Freud argued that, on the contrary, violence is always integral to the political economies of states: it is just that usually we do not see it manifested so explicitly, so spectacularly, and confusingly visible—so in our faces (and directed at

83

the faces of others, as in the case of Shamima Begum). In other words, wartime is bewildering because it brings to the surface a violence that was already there.

The wars that Europe, the United States, and the Anglosphere fight today are of a different order to the wars of the twentieth century. Contemporary warfare takes place in slow time (the so-called 'forever war'), often against abstractions ('terror') and pseudo-states rather than legitimate nations. Proxy wars are our preferred medium. We like to watch. If our everyday fantasies of violence—such as using images of Shamima Begum for target practice—have become banal in this process it is because at some level wartime has now become our habitual time. Bewilderment is the new normal. Nonetheless, there are two lessons from Freud's description of the everyday violence of wartime in the last century that might help us navigate the confusion of the present.

First, his psychoanalytic spin on the observation that violence is neither simply something that happens 'over there' or which 'other people' do but rather that it is stitched into the fabric of politics and governance, and so into the way we see the world. As Étienne Balibar has argued, citizenship is the political regulation of violence.[6] The logic here, as Freud keenly appreciated, was first laid out by the seventeenth-century philosopher, Thomas Hobbes when he explained how it is that in order to have self-sovereignty, we need to surrender to the sovereignty of the state. Citizenship is the club you get to join in exchange for relinquishing the right to survive and prosper by tearing the guys next door to bits. Freud's contribution to this argument was to point out that psychically this violence never goes away entirely. You relinquish the right to be violent, but not the desire: hence violence's availability for political exploitation. Citizenship itself, in other words, is haunted by the violence upon which it is founded, which may be one reason why the images and feelings that cluster around de-citizenship, such as in the Begum and other high profile cases, are so particularly freighted.

Until recently, de-citizenship belonged to history books of twentieth-century ethno-nationalism, to the Nuremberg laws, fascism, and the pre-history of genocide. The past twenty years, however, have witnessed an increased willingness of states to use exclusion as a political tool. In 2002, the UK Labour government introduced the Nationality, Immigration and Asylum Act. The act made it possible to detain asylum seekers and migrants indefinitely. It also granted the Home Secretary the power to strip a person of their citizenship 'if the secretary of state is satisfied that the person has done anything seriously prejudicial to the vital interests of the United Kingdom or a British overseas territory.' At first, nobody much noticed the new policy. Migrants were quietly shipped into quietly built private detention centres that mushroomed silently next to airports and just off motorways in the 2000s. Very few people were stripped of citizenship. As novelist Kamila Shamsie observed in an article published three months before Shamima Begum's case hit the headlines, de-citizenship increased dramatically with the rise of ISIS and the emergence of a decidedly unsympathetic category of persons who seemed to be self-evidently doing things prejudicial to the United Kingdom:

> [I]n 2013, 18 people were deprived of citizenship, a huge increase from the six of the previous two years. In 2014, the number was 23. In July 2017 the Times reported that the number of those who had their citizenship revoked so far that year was already over 40. And yes, the rise in numbers occurred at the same time that increased numbers of British citizens first went to join Islamic

State, and then tried to return after the collapse of Isis's so-called caliphate. And yes, that makes it a little difficult to sympathise.[7]

As Shamsie argues, stripping people of citizenship saves the state the bother of legally demonstrating evidence of that prejudicial action, but then again that was precisely why the 2002 act had left the Home Secretary's grounds for banishment so open to interpretation in the first place.

From a long historical viewpoint there is nothing especially new or, some would even say, necessarily alarming here. States have always made laws and used violence in order to protect their security. National security nearly always trumps the rights of members of terror groups. The 'confusion', to borrow Freud's word, sets in once this exclusion both legitimates and segues into other kinds of violence: when everyday violence is appropriated both for the state and, as such, potentially at least, for the sake of violence itself. The act of stripping a person of their nationality transforms a former citizen into a stranger and enemy for everybody to witness. It is not just a piece of law or policy to protect the nation: it is a spectacle, a fantasy, a kind of target practice. The risk is not simply that the stripping of citizenship might be viewed as disproportionate, lacking in empathy or mercy or, as in the Begum case, racist, Islamophobic and misogynist (although it could well be all these things too), but that when the state nails its colours to collective fantasy so blatantly, judgement (to recall Freud's other word) and discrimination get much harder.

From this perspective, debating the legality of de-citizenship only partly deals with the problem of bewilderment. The new human rights regime set in place following the Second World War worked hard to ensure that no-one could be deprived of citizenship again. Citizenship was understood as a right, not a privilege to be granted or withheld. The 1948 British Nationality Act granted citizenship to all former colonial subjects, and ended the practice of stripping women of their British nationality as soon as they married a foreigner (this law was one of the reasons Virginia Woolf declared herself as having 'no country' in *Three Guineas*). As Arendt pointed out, to be stateless is to be denied even the right to have rights. International law is quite clear that only those with someplace else to be a citizen can be legally expelled, even as subsequent national laws have fudged around this requirement. Just now we are clearly crossing an accepted threshold. In Begum's case some have challenged the legality of the Home Office's decision, but whether or not the UK acted legally is a correctly contested point.[8] The second lesson we might draw from Freud's bewilderment is less about legitimacy *per se* than about the social and political organization of legal violence in frantic times. The issue is less about the law itself, than about what we imagine we're doing with the law.

As the American jurist Robert Cover argued in a classic essay from 1986, legal interpretations and judgments are always potentially violent in self-evidently literal ways: somebody is going to get punished. That is the whole point. Even as legal and political decision-making takes place at one remove from that violence, it remains the case that political-legal worlds, like the nation states they support, are built and maintained by putting human bodies on the line.[9] Just because we've lost the taste for public execution and torture does not alter the fact that because someone, property, institution, nation, or idea has been hurt, so somebody will also be hurt in response. Banishment, as philosophers have long pointed out, demarcates the line between citizens and their others—which may be another reason why images associated with de-citizenship are so overdetermined. The stripping of citizenship, legally and politically, is a limit experience for all concerned.

This might also be why the twin of the expelled citizen is the figure with whom she has become most associated with today: the fanatical martyr. Martyrs, as Cover noted in his 1986 essay, repudiate the normative world of law both by willingly bearing its violence on their bodies and by ostentatiously performing their commitment to the possibility (however wrong) of a higher law. Martyrs do not play by the game—or rather, they play the violence of the game all too well. Martyrs shove violence back in our faces. Let me burn on your stake, says Joan of Arc: this horror is the result of earthly laws, not God's. Martyrs disturb, Cover suggests, because they give the lie to the illusion that the law is set apart from the violence it also seeks to legislate against. Like the expelled citizen, they trouble the very boundaries they are supposed to demarcate.

If we run Freud and Cover together here, we could argue that, as with more conventional wars, violent extremism is bewildering not simply because it is beyond moral norms and customs, but because it drags out into the open disconcerting evidence of the underlying violence upon which our political lives together are built. 'We are at loss', Freud wrote in 1915, as to the value of the judgements we form. The presence of everyday violence challenges how we think about the world, the categories we use to understand it, and our moral responsibility to it. Finding targets is an efficient way of circumventing the psychic and political difficulties of that responsibility—it also how we keep the violence going. When the management of the shooting range decided that

88

it would be fun to turn Shamima Begum's image into a target, they were confirming that what began as a war on terror in the West is now the violence of the everyday.

How we might find our moral and imaginative bearings amid this everyday violence was the subject of Kamila Shamsie's award-winning and extraordinarily prescient 2017 novel *Home Fire*, published a full two years before the Shamima Begum case, and just as a succession of British Home Secretaries were developing a taste for selective de-citizenship. The novel is a retelling of the Antigone story, so (as we saw with Virginia Woolf and Simone Weil in Chapter Three) we are back in the tradition here of modern women writers who use Antigone's stubbornness to challenge the moral and political compass of man-made laws. In Shamsie's version, a sister attempts to repatriate the body of her dead twin brother from Pakistan where it had been deported after he had been stripped of his British citizenship. As with Begum, in the novel, Aneeka's brother Parvaiz (also a Londoner) had joined ISIS in his teens. The twist is that Aneeka is in love with the son of the Home Secretary, a Muslim, who is keen to demonstrate his Britishness through his uncompromising use of de-citizenship.

As Ankhi Mukhjerjee has argued, by casting Aneeka/Antigone at the intersection of law and politics, the novel theatricalizes the sheer—and terrifying—excessiveness of the racialized violence of the everyday.[10] In this, *Home Fire* understands the contemporary power of images to create moral, political and categorial whirlwinds as well as Freud did in the last century. In the final chapter, under the gaze of the world's cameras, Aneeka/Antigone sits in a park in Karachi, keeping vigil over the ice-packed rotting corpse of her brother. In the ultimate scene, the Home Secretary's son, sacrificing his ties to his father, the law, and to Britain, runs toward her. As he runs, he is grabbed from behind and a suicide belt is strapped to him—an unwilling martyr to a cause that was never his own. Here is that scene in full:

> But everyone is running, towards this exit or that, screams and voices raised to God, who else can save them now? One camera-man, a veteran of carnage, stops at the edge of the park, beyond the blast radius as best he can judge, turns his lens onto the new empti-ness of the field. The woman has stood up now. The man with the explosives around his waist holds up both his hand to stop her coming to him. *Run!* He shouts. *Get away from me, run!* And run she does, crashing right into him, a judder of the camera as the man holding it on his shoulder flinches in expectation of a blast. At first the man in the navy shirt struggles, but her arms are around him, she whispers something, and he stops. She rests her cheek against his, he drops his head to kiss her shoulder. For a moment they are two lovers in a park, under an ancient tree, sun-dappled, beautiful and at peace.[11]

As Mukherjee points out, Aneeka's actions, her love, make her not of this world: she is a 'sovereign subject yet to come.' But as the sublime cinematic framing of this passage also makes clear, we are as yet in arrested time. The cameraman expertly points his gaze at the empty field, waiting for flesh to explode. But Shamsie denies us that violence and gives us instead an image of two lovers in a park. This is as accurate a representation of our modern tragedy as I have read in the past five years. To be suspended between a vio-lence that is now both extreme and normalized and something other, perhaps a kind of love that we have yet to work out how to turn into politics: this, seems to be exactly where we are just now.

Shamsie's lesson echoes Freud's as well as Sophocles'. When the state starts to use violence for the sake of violence itself, it trig-gers something latent in our politics that is difficult to comprehend or contain. If wartime is now our habitual time, we urgently need to find ways of attending to this everyday violence that depend on neither denial or displacement, nor banishment, nor on using images of young women as target practice. 'He didn't know how to break out of these currents of history, how to shake free of the demons he had attached to his own heels,' Shamsie writes of the bemused and deluded teenage ISIS recruit in her novel.[12] The danger now is that our democracies are now also at a loss as to how to shake the demons attached to their own feet.

CHAPTER SIX

SURVIVAL TIME/
HUMAN TIME

Hannah Arendt and Behrouz Boochani

Being a refugee is neither a noun nor a verb, but a stutter in time-space, always repeating.

Chris Abani[1]

The world of refugees is a vast narrative landscape.

Aleksander Hemon[2]

Is 'being a refugee' to also become a stutter in time-space, as Chris Abani suggests? A category of person always on the edge of speaking something, going somewhere, being someone, but imprisoned in a grammar that refuses development and even time itself? Or, alternatively, is the world of refugees, as Aleksander Hemon puts it, a 'vast narrative landscape', full of people and words, stories and becoming, a place, and a time, unimaginable to those who live in the lands of citizenship? My answer in this chapter is that it could be both, but that we need to adjust our ways of thinking about the temporalities of statelessness in order to see it.[3]

If we don't tend to stutter in the time-space of the nation, this is because we are so familiar with its genre of time. The nation is always here and now because it was always once lost and so is forever being found. 'Having common glories in the past and a will to continue them in the present; having made great things together and wishing to make them again', as Ernest Renan famously put it in 1882.[4] The nation's mythic potentialities unfurl back to the imaginings of a lost past and look forward to a redemptive future identity. There is a familiarity about the times of nationalism, even though, as now, the boorish loquaciousness of some of its adherents often points to an anxiety about its future durability.

In a fascinating short afterword to a 2008 special issue of the journal *Contemporary Literature*, literary critic Ian Baucom described how it is otherwise with the nation's elder sibling—the state. The state has a much older, and a much 'thinner grammar of time.'[5] The state just is, and we are just in its present. It is as though, Baucom notes, the state has somehow put the question of time— of different histories, futures, beginnings and endings—'outside of itself'. It's perfectly possible to invent new genres of political life outside nationalism, as utopian writers and political thinkers have been doing ever since the nation state emerged, but thinking of another kind of time outside the state is almost unimaginable. It is only *almost* unimaginable because in the deep time of the state there was always—and is always—the threat of never-ending brutal war, of each against each, which, as Hobbes explained, our contract with state sovereignty was intended to banish. As Baucom points out, this contract was also temporal in nature; a 'guarantee that the unimaginable past will not invade the present and has been banished from the future.'[6]

Writing in 2008, Baucom identified two developments that were threatening to undermine that contract. First, the emergence of new global forms of power changed the ways we thought about the spaces of the world. The nation state appeared to shrink. A somewhat shrivelled ghost of its former self, its frailty made the unimaginable past that bit more imaginable. Secondly, at the same moment, refugees and migrants fleeing failed and failing states were also starting to remind the world that it was, after all, frighteningly easy to find yourself in the non-time of stateless-ness. Ten years on, the shrivelled ghosts have pumped themselves up into cartoon strongmen, and the spaces of real and potential statelessness have blossomed in the cracks between nations—in border zones, in off-shore migrant and prison camps, in unmarked buildings on the edges of airfields, in shipping containers, in the ironic 'living the dream' photo captions on Facebook pages between home and wherever. The stuttering we can hear now is the sound of survival time. It also is the sound of a collective historical failure—a repeated click and tick of the menace of life outside the time of the state.

But this is only, I think, half the story. To see statelessness as the non-time of the nation state is to concede too much to its historical and interpretative authority, even as, more often than not, refu-gees and migrants especially have no choice but to concede to its political authority. The scholar Gary Wilder has written of a 'methodological nationalism' that persists in postcolonial studies, as though we can only look out at the world from within the tem-poralities of the nation state.[7] A similar methodological nationalism is often also present in the way we frame and think about refugees and migrants. Often too often quick to consign the experience of being refugee to trauma—to an experience shatteringly and uncannily out of 'our' time—we have missed some of the narra-tive continuities in the refiguring of human time as witnessed, thought and written about by those who have survived conditions of historical, existential, and political statelessness. My two examples in this chapter are Hannah Arendt and the Iranian-Kurdish writer and political philosopher Behrouz Boochani, who was held at the Australian detention centre on Manus Island between 2013 until its closure in 2017. He then spent two more years on the island, before finally leaving in the autumn of 2019.[†] Too ready to reduce the forms and genres of forced displacement and imprisonment to individual testimony, we have also failed to appreciate how writers of the placeless condition have transformed the poetics of the past, present, and future of political life from, by necessity, outside the rhythms of the nation state. By not thinking hard enough about what it means to exist in the nation state's 'non-time', we have yet to understand the relation between the endless work of survival and the persistence, and struggle, of keeping time human despite inhuman conditions.

This chapter falls into two parts. In the first part, I return to Arendt and the mid-twentieth century: not just to her now famous analysis of statelessness, but to the ways in which thinking and being outside the nation state surface in her later writing on the human condition, human time, historiography and the politics of storytelling. In the second part, I turn to Boochani's extraordinary book *No Friend but the Mountains*, first published in 2018. Written on Manus Island, it is a text distinguished by—among very many things—its determination to keep human time going in the face of its systematic destruction by the Australian state. Common to both thinkers is the recognition that the persistence of totalitarian forms in modern history requires the development of counter-temporal and historical forms of agency. Put more simply, their

[†] At the time of writing, Boochani remains in New Zealand where he arrived, on a one-month visa, in November 2019.

response to being thrown into an 'unimaginable' time beyond the state is not simply to demand re-entry into its temporalities, nor is it simply to stutter, but rather to reclaim the political potentialities of human time through the acts of thinking and writing.

Human Time

Arendt's analysis of how the twentieth-century European state finally succumbed to its own racism and nationalism to reproduce colonial levels of brutality within its own borders is now well-known. The refugees of the early and mid-twentieth century came with a message, she argued in *The Origins of Totalitarianism* (1951): that the world thought nothing of the abstract nakedness of merely being human.[8] What were fondly imagined as 'human rights' turned out to mean only the rights of nationals and citizens and, as such, were somewhat frail defenders of life and liberty for the forcibly displaced. While Arendt's critique of nationalism is well understood, less commented upon is her equally implacable rejection of state sovereignty.[9] When she says, famously, that only a political community in which one can appear and speak can guarantee the right to have rights, she does not simply mean that if we could somehow strip the state of its nationalist narratives things might work out better.[10] She also means that the contract we have with the state is itself part of the problem. 'The freedom of one man, or a group, or a body politic can be purchased only at the price of the freedom, i.e., the sovereignty, of all others,' she wrote in 'What is Freedom?'

Where men wish to be sovereign, as individuals or as organized groups, they must submit to the oppression of the will, be this the individual will with which I force myself, or the "general will" of an organized group. If men wish to be free it is precisely sovereignty they must renounce.[11]

In the context of Baucom's arguments, we might say that Arendt positions herself in the 'unimaginable' non-time of the state. This wasn't just a theoretical move. For eighteen years of her life as a stateless person, statelessness was also the legal and historical category from which she viewed the world. One of her former students once told me that just before her death, Arendt lamented that the full story of her generation of refugees had yet to be told fully. But in many ways, and not just in the obvious texts, she never stopped telling that story.

This was also a story about time. In an essay written eight years after her death, Arendt's friend Paul Ricœur argued that *The Human Condition* (1958) was, in part at least, a radical attempt to re-think human time from beyond, before, and after the times of modern totalitarianism. The text, he argued, describes 'the most enduring features of the *temporal* condition of man—those which are the least vulnerable to the vicissitudes of the modern age.'[12] Ricœur was interested in how Arendt affirmed 'human time'— both our chronological lives and our experience of time—as against modern forms and genres of time, including those of the totalitarian state and nationalism, and, importantly, the forms of history telling that enabled them.[13] In Ricœur's reading, Arendt's famous three categories of human life—labour, work, and action—are also responses to the temporal conditions of modern man. Thus, labouring is what we do simply to survive; its time is transitory, as what we need to live we need in our lifetimes, today and not tomorrow. What we work at, 'human artifice,' by contrast, endures in time. This is why the reduction of work to sheer labour is also an attack on human time: to labour simply to stay alive is to be denied human durability. The labour and death camps of *The Origins of Totalitarianism* are not far away here. Neither are Boochani's later descriptions of the endless labour of queuing simply in order to eat in strictly-controlled groups of five in Manus Prison camp:

> *The logic of five*
> *Five people follow on from five people/*
> *...*
> *Human agency is subdued to the number five.*[14]

Outside the modern detention camp, and back home in the capitalist nation state, the transformation of the results of work into consumables has also reduced work to labour. When all we make is for consumption, we have effectively trashed what makes us human. In terms of temporalities of the human condition, the camp and consumer capitalism are two sides of the same coin. Only if the distinction between work and labour can be maintained, Arendt argues, can we continue to live in a world of our making such that the human condition can endure. As Ricœur summarizes:

> It's within a humanized world that man is born and dies. For the same reason, the span of time between birth and death deserves to be called *Bio* and no-longer *Zoë*. Life, then, is full of events 'which ultimately can be told as a story, establish a biography.'[15]

This is why Arendt's third category, action, and particularly action as a form of storytelling, is so important to Ricœur. Storytelling actualizes human time. But this is very different from the self-memorialization of the makers of history. No-one is simply the author or the subject of even their own life-story:

the stories, the results of action and speech, reveal an agent, but this agent is not an author or producer. Somebody began it and is its subject in the two-fold sense of the word, namely, as its author and its sufferer, but nobody is its author.[16]

'Nobody is its author.' The subjects of what Arendt calls the 'great storybook of mankind' are not sovereign subjects, but both authors *and* sufferers. This is what guarantees plurality as well as immortality: no one (body of people, individual, or nation state) is buying the freedom to live on in the future at the cost of the oppression of others.

This suggests a very different kind of temporal contract from the one Baucom identifies as pertaining to the sovereign state. There is no 'non-time' that needs to be banished to an unimaginable deep history, nor, indeed, to the contemporary blind-sites of statelessness, which, likewise, are both seen and not seen. Rather, if storytelling is an action that resists the elimination of human time, we can also perhaps think about Arendt as telling a refugee or survival story here. As much as it is a description of life, *The Human Condition* is also a text about how to survive the placeless condition. Life itself and surviving placelessness may yet, of course, end up being the same thing, as the corona virus and the climate emergency are perhaps beginning to teach us.

Arendt is often criticized for banishing certain kinds of life (the private, the social) from the *polis*, and so closing down the possibilities of other kinds of political agency and action. But, as I have argued elsewhere, she never wholly stops writing from the perspective of statelessness.[17] Time and time again in her writing, Arendt affirms the potential for action even in conditions of utmost, and abject, passive suffering. Something (Ricœur would probably call it human time) always has to keep moving in both her thought and her writing.

In *The Human Condition*, a text that often seems determined to strip itself of history and context, this restlessness plays out on a linguistic level too. Words are never quite at home. 'The human sense of reality demands that men actualize the sheer passive givenness of their being,' Arendt writes at one point. Note how using three words to describe one experience—'sheer passive givenness'—render it a kind of agency. There is an awful lot of activity going on in this description of passivity, here and elsewhere. The human demand for actualization cannot change conditions of enforced passivity, she continues, but it can 'articulate and call into full existence' what 'otherwise they would have to suffer passively anyhow.'[18] This surely is also what Arendt's own writing is constantly demonstrating: articulate passivity. In another strikingly strange circumlocutory passage, she writes about the 'capacity for action' as harbouring 'within it certain potentialities which enable it to survive the disabilities of non-sovereignty.'[19] Is statelessness a 'disability of non-sovereignty'? If so, we can perhaps now read those 'disabilities of non-sovereignty' in a twofold way: as at once referring to the historical and political condition of non-sovereignty as produced by, and in the times of, the nation state; and, more quietly, as a form of surviving the same condition of statelessness that contains within it the potential for action.

Just to be clear, what Arendt is emphatically not saying—and neither am I—is that the deathly labour of surviving enforced statelessness is in any way or means good for anybody or anything, in any political, human, or planetary terms whatsoever. What she *is* saying is that if you turn the telescope around the other way and stop seeing statelessness as some small faraway island at some temporal and geographical distance from the anxieties of the modern nation state, and start seeing it instead as where the question of human survival—and perhaps even human time itself—begins today, things start to look different.

Where do you write from when you are being banished from what looks like time itself? That was one of Arendt's abiding questions. Arendt thought that the genres of modern history had squeezed out a place from which it was even possible to imagine being outside the modern nation state, which is why so much of her own history-writing was self-confessedly unconventional. As she put it in introduction to *The Origins of Totalitarianism*, because there are some kinds of history that you want to destroy, rather than preserve, storytelling needs to stay creative. Arendt wanted to destroy both totalitarian thinking and the genres of historiography that supported it. When modern (read Western) man decided he was, after all, not in a collective storybook of contingent happenings made alongside other forms of life, but the sole author of history, he also lost his place in human time. Storytelling became less about actions, suffering, contingency, as 'the historical fate of nations, their rise and fall, where the particular actions and events were engulfed in a whole.'[20] Because human lives became accountable only to those big narratives—as process, history, nature, and so forth—so too, eventually, did the assumptions that drove them (in Arendt's words) end up being 'as mad' as they pleased, producing 'facts which are then "objectively" true.'[21] 'Facts' such as those paraded in racism. 'Objective truths' such as the necessity for prison and detention camps.

Torn from human time, modern history conspired with narratives of totalitarian thinking to the point at which 'quite literally' everything became possible, 'not only in the realm of ideas but in the field of reality itself.'[22] As the unimaginable became real in fascist Europe, the temporal contract between the sovereign state and citizens too started to weaken. By the 1940s, the brutish inhuman existence that sovereignty had supposedly banished had recreated itself in the *Lagers*, prison, detention, and death camps, right at the heart of the European nation state itself.

No Friend but the Mountains

Half-way through her essay, 'The Concept of History' (published in the same year as *The Human Condition*, 1958), Arendt quotes four lines from Rainer Maria Rilke's tenth poem in the cycle 'The Remains of Count C.W'. Denver Lindley's translation of these lines reads:

> Here even the mountains only seem to rest under the light of the stars; they are slowly, secretly devoured by time; nothing is forever, immortality has fled the world to find an uncertain abode in darkness of the human heart that still has the capacity to remember and to say: forever.[23]

Nothing is forever. Even the mountains seem temporary. Human time now resides only in the human heart. Arendt, as she well knew, was writing under the shadow of an already floundering European cosmopolitanism. Mass statelessness, with its grammar of immobility, imprisonment and stasis, had already begun to undermine the poetics of exile offered by Rilke. Today, the 'soft exile' of the cosmopolitan writer is embarrassingly inadequate to the realities of displacement, deportation, and imprisonment. By contrast, Behrouz Boochani's writing comes directly (literally) from the histories of statelessness and colonial and postcolonial appropriation that Arendt was beginning to analyse. Like Arendt and Rilke, Boochani finds a temporal touchpoint in the vulnerable but seeming permanence of the mountains—they are his only friends, linking the past to present, the outside to the inside of the camp. Boochani's mountains are those he grew up on in Kurdistan—the nation that is not allowed to be a state—and which he remembers; and the mountain on Manus Island, which offer both a refuge and viewpoint from which, with patient precision, he documents and analyses the slow sovereign violence of what he describes, after the work of the feminist theologian Elisabeth Schüssler Fiorenza, as the 'Kyriarchal System'.

Arendt predicted that forms of totalitarianism would persist in the world long after the demise of totalitarian states. Boochani and his translator and collaborator Omid Tofighian demonstrate how totalitarian thinking has migrated from inside the twentieth-century state to provide the logic of contemporary border control in the twenty-first. As with its twentieth-century variants, a mix of totalitarian ideology and terror work both the system of the detention camp and the politics that enables the citizens of Western democracies to somehow stomach what is being done in their name. Arendt argued that one of the characteristic features of modern totalitarianism was the 'boomeranging' back to the European nation state of colonial administrative practices of brutal dehumanization. Boochani reveals that it is precisely the colonial aspects of totalitarianism that have endured into the twenty-first century.

The racist legacies of Australian settler-colonialism proved to be a fertile seedbed for the early experiments in border control that were begun in the 1990s and that have since been rolled out to

Europe and the United States. Under colonial rule, it was labour, resources and capital; now it is the political economy of refugees and migrants that is outsourced overseas in dodgy trade-offs based on implicit and increasingly explicit racist thinking. Whereas in the twentieth century the point of the totalitarian camp was to eliminate those deemed enemies of the state, the point of the Kyriarchal System is *refoulement*: 'Returning the refugee prisoners to the land from which they came.' Not since Primo Levi's accounts of how the Nazi *Lager* was designed to create the terror necessary for prisoners to collude in their own dehumanization has the organization of violence been described with such controlled, and devastating, accuracy:

> Hatred runs through every prisoner. In the prison hatred makes prisoners more insular. The weight of hared is so intense that the prisoners will suddenly collapse on a dark night and give up resisting…surrender to a system that induces and amplifies hatred… and accept refoulement.[24]

The obscenity of industrial genocide has been replaced with the illegality of *refoulement*. *Refoulement* was prohibited by the 1951 Refugee Convention.

The suppression of human time is intrinsic to the aims of the refugee regime in Manus prison. Life is reduced to the labour of survival. The endless queues; the waiting lists for specialist medical attention when all that is ever available is paracetamol; the appointment with the Godot-like dentist who never arrives (and whose absence means that Boochani seeks relief in the excruciating, but effective, cauterising methods of the Manus islanders); the tobacco trade likewise designed to create need, not relief; the rationing of telephone calls home: all these are 'mad' in the sense that Arendt would have recognized. It is a madness administered with the goal of making it so intolerable to exist in this timeless zone of never-ending affliction that the refugees will eventually willingly spring back 'to where they came from' if only to re-enter some kind of temporal existence. And if they go back, or at least so goes the fantasy, so too might the familiar temporalities of the nation state be restored.

In Baucom's terms, we could say that the Australian state, like the United States, the United Kingdom, and most of the nations that make up the European Union, is attempting to restore its temporal equilibrium. As this involves constantly recreating its own 'non-time' in the present—that is, reconstructing versions of the very past and future that it was supposed to banish in the field of reality—this, as is rapidly becoming apparent, is something of a self-defeating strategy.

Even to write, in this context, is to seize back work—and so human time—from the dead-time of labouring-to-survive. Boochani wrote his book in the form of texts and WhatsApp messages. This is no agentless refugee testimony. Nor is it fiction. Those yet to read *No Friend but the Mountains* frequently refer to is as either a 'memoir' or a 'novel'. In reality, Boochani, like Arendt, is inventing a new genre of writing out of historical, political, and existential necessity. From its opening descriptions of the terror of crossing from Indonesia to Australian waters, two things are made clear in his text: first, that human time will not be surrendered; and second, that the act of keeping time in play depends not on the heroism of the individual author—there is no triumphing over adversity, no bright new future forged from toil and suffering, absolutely no redemption here—but on the creation of a temporal agency that is at once collective and contingent. 'All our hopes are focused on one tiny luminous point in the distance,' Boochani writes of the refugees' journey in the too-small, too-rickety boat: 'A common will takes form in solidarity and struggle. What is the connection between our survival and reaching that insignificant bright spot?' he asks.[25]

It is precisely any connection to the future that is denied by the Australian state. Survival time, not human time, comes to define solidarity and struggle. Even so, right from the off, Boochani's writing claims time for those on the boat, for refugees, for those about to be imprisoned, and for himself. 'The path of death and the flow of life are both made manifest in our bodies;' he writes. It is the 'empty vessel' that is 'subject to destruction', not the flow of human time. 'I imagine myself looking back from an unknown place beyond' he continues—'myself looking back at me. I see a dead body, but with eyes still alert, struggling to survive.'[26] I see myself surviving: might it not be, recalling Ricœur's reading of Arendt, that to survive is also to actualize yourself in narrative time?

It both is and is not. Like Arendt's writing, Boochani's refuses to valorize either statelessness or stateless time. As with *The Human Condition*, perhaps the most unaccommodating writing in her œuvre, *No Friend but the Mountain* consciously pushes against a language that might naturalize the political and historical conditions of its telling.

Boochani's collaborator and translator Omid Tofighian has written of the 'horrific surrealism' of his writing.[27] I think this is right, and that the otherworldliness of this text is partly where the originality of its politics is located. Nothing and nobody on Manus can ever be quite itself—the flowers on the island, for example, only 'resemble chamomile'; the mountains are both those of Boochani's Kurdish home and those of the island; his fellow prisoners are recognizable only by their traits: Maysam The Whore, the Gentle Giant, Father-of-the-Months-Old-Child. This writing does not so much stutter arrested in time and space, to go back to Abani, it shimmers between realities.

Boochani imagines himself looking back 'from an unknown place beyond.' Edward Said wrote of Conrad's writing that its elaborate strangeness communicated the twentieth-century exile's sense that he could never convey his existence to an uncomprehending and hostile world.[28] Boochani's 'horrific surrealism' likewise speaks from 'an unknown place beyond' the time-space of the Western nation state. But there is an important difference too. Whereas Conrad's encounter with the destructive element brought him face-to-face with human solitude, Boochani writes not (or at least, not only) to a hostile world, but from Kurdistan, Iran, from the sea, from Manus Prison, from Manus Island and its people, from networks of transnationalist activism. In Arendtian terms, we could say that the actions and encounters recorded in in his book reveal a kind of agency, but it is not only Boochani's agency as its author and producer.

This is not only a book about the extermination of human time: it is also study of what Elena Fiddian-Qasmiyeh has described as the 'poetics of undisclosed care' that exists between those trapped in the grey zones of contemporary statelessness.[29] At every turn, other lives and life forms connect in this writing. In a shared glance at a child across the refugee boat, for example: 'My eyes follow the child – my eyes, the eyes of a foreigner, together with the loving eyes of the mother, both stitched to this infant's little body. Our concerned gazes are transfixed by this child.'[30] In an obscure moaning that at once comes from the mountain and Behrouz's mouth: 'Maybe we share the same affliction?'[31] In Fox Prison, Boochani discovers that a woman and her daughters there before him have left poems to mark their presence on the walls and ceiling:

> I don't know why I feel the presence of that family when I read the poetry/
> I don't know why I feel the presence of the wife and her daughters when I read the poetry/
> I feel their presence and their beauty/
> They were lively and active/
> They were living life.[32]

It is not just human presence that Boochani is connecting with here, but human time. The family have left him their story which he, in turn, is telling. This storytelling—between authors and sufferers—claims the right of biography from within the deadtime of Manus Prison. To keep the narrative threads between birth and death, past, present, and future connected is to defy the non-time of the camp. This is also why, in another scene, Boochani carefully describes how the prisoners attempt to ensure that Father-of-the-Months-Old-Child can defeat the endless waiting of the telephone queue to speak to his own dying father. They fail. But the point is that by trying (by acting, Arendt would say), the possibility of a human world in which men and women are born and die—in which biography is possible—endures.

Boochani is giving us more than the Hobbesian fantasy that haunts the ever-more murderous politics of contemporary border control. Like Arendt, he is allowing us to glimpse another kind of time. His book ends with a staging of tragedy which Arendt, I think, would have appreciated. The prisoners riot. Suddenly we glimpse a world where the men can assume their roles, to be seen, heard, to act: *The Comedian embodied an actor on stage/The Comedian embodied a poet/*'; 'The Hero... and his roar'. Like the Greek poets who Arendt loved because of the way they recorded the spontaneous acts that made freedom possible, Boochani captures the moment for prosperity—for, exactly, another time. When inevitably the lights go down—the prison authorities kill the generator and quash the rebellion—amid all the noise, one sound distinguishes itself from the chaos:

> *A familiar sound from a forlorn point/*
> *The sound pierced my ear like the wind/*
> *It rested on my heart/*
> *It rested on my heart/*
> *It was the sound of someone who uttered in Kurdish 'dālega!/*
> *It was the sound of someone who cried 'Mother!'*[33]

A footnote informs us that *dālega* is the 'word for mother in the Kurdish Feyli dialect'. Whereas in strict legal terms most of the refugees on Manus, as elsewhere, are only potentially stateless, the Feyli Kurds who live on the border between Iran and Iraq are comprehensively stateless, recognized by nobody. They really do live in stateless time. But in the end, I do not think that cry is only a lament uttered from the deep history of statelessness—the non-time a currently out-of-control nationalism is manically, uselessly, attempting to banish. The cry is also the sound of a voice, a child, a son, a man, with a life and a biography, inserting himself in time at the precise moment that it is human time itself he is being denied.

CHAPTER SEVEN

CONCLUSION

Hannah Arendt in Baddawi

Composing her teaching notes for her course on 'Political Experience in the Twentieth Century' at the New School in New York in 1968, Hannah Arendt rehearsed how she was going to explain to her political science students why they were going to be reading a lot of literature. The course was ambitious. Arendt wanted her American students to try to capture the experience of living in Europe under fascism and totalitarianism. She didn't want explanations, theories, or grand narratives about how it was that Europe had finally sunk into a human rights quagmire of its own making. She wanted real thinking about what it was like to experience total war, forced displacement, imprisonment, and industrial genocide. And that was why the novels and poems were required reading alongside the political theory and history books:

> We try to recapture experiences, but not those of the makers of history, but of those who were its 'sufferers', by which I mean no more than: those who were not in charge.[1]

Arendt did not want her students to be particularly creative. She did not want them to feel bad about a historical experience that was radically unlike their own. She wanted to teach them how to think about history from the perspective of those who are not in charge. Arendt's literary reading list was as pale, male, and Western as any taught in the US in the 1950s and 1960s. Her own capacity for thinking about the experience of other people, particularly African-Americans was sometimes wanting. Yet the idea of beginning with literature in order to really think about what it means to suffer oppression is a powerful one that, I believe, we're not yet done with. Arendt would have had no truck with the patronizing idea of 'giving voice' to those who were suffering. If she wanted to think about history from the perspective of the powerless, it was to upend comfortable assumptions about how we tell history in the first place. 'And since we are working in the medium of history, though seen through literature, we are somewhat confronted with the all the puzzling questions that usually are dealt with in the Philosophy', she explained. 'There is another way of writing history.'

If one post-war history of human rights has run into trouble lately it is because liberal sentiment has shown itself badly, and sometimes fatally, inadequate, to the task at hand. Co-opting literature in defence of the liberal imagination, at this point in the twenty-first century, feels a bit like flogging a rather timid pony that once dreamt of being a pretty impressive horse. Yes, the novel form is a brilliant medium for freedom, judgement, and dissent. Yes, writing plays out the multiple ironies of living with others in an atrocious world. Yes, sometimes in a poem you can feel the world open up to reveal ways of being with one another so exquisite that you have to draw breath. But if literature is doing all these amazing and beautiful things merely to prop up our sense of powerless anguish, then it is really not doing very much at all.

Critical-creative writing coming from the rightless places and times of history, on the other hand, has been doing something else for quite some time. This isn't particularly grand stuff. At even their least ambitious, many writers have been doing what litera- ture has been doing for a long time, which is to reclaim human dignity back from the anonymity and indignity of inhuman his- torical processes. The narratives of the sufferers of history survive if, and sometimes only because, they are recorded, written, and so kept in history by people who also happen to be really good writers. The problem, as anti-colonial and feminist thinkers have been tirelessly pointing out for a long time now, is that, because we are still struggling with dominant philosophies of history, not enough of this writing is allowed to find its place in the world. It is as though we have been writing two literary histories of human rights at once: one still bumps along hoping that enough moral sympathy can be generated to make the world a better place; the other is writing a history of suffering and survival that has yet to be archived or recognized.

Few writers have taught me more about the poetry of precarity and survival lately than the poet Yousif M. Qasmiyeh, with whom I have been working on an interdisciplinary project on refugee hosting in Lebanon, Jordan, and Turkey, for the past five years, *Refugee Hosts*.[2] Now living and working in the UK, Qasmiyeh was born and raised in Baddawi, a Palestinian refugee camp, on the northern border of Lebanon. Created in 1955, home to approxi- mately 40,000 'established' Palestinian refugees, over the years the camp has created communities and cultures and endured civil war and lawlessness. Since 2011, the people of Baddawi have also hosted thousands of refugees fleeing the war in Syria, as well as from Iraq and Kurdistan. Baddawi, and other places on the frontline of survival, is where the modern meanings of human rights are being worked out just now, on the ground, collectively, locally, in acts of 'refugee-refugee humanitarianism' that Elena Fiddian-Qasmiyeh, Qasmiyeh's partner and the project lead of Refugee Hosts, has judiciously described as 'an undisclosed poetics of care.'[3]

Baddawi is a comparatively small Palestinian camp, so the physical impact of new refugees is not hard to see. Its architecture has been squeezed upward over the past ten years: concrete scrambled onto concrete; new homes have been made out of courtyards and balconies; vegetable gardens improvised wherever the sun might catch. In an extraordinary sequence of poems, Qasmiyeh has taken this density, this crowdedness, and turned it into a means of talking about how the largely understated, almost invisible, work of memory, care and survival, gets done when people are suddenly and violently pushed together. These poems are as dense as Baddawi itself. Like the camp's narrow alleyways, they are dark: it is hard to see clearly what is happening on the page in front of you. But they are also poems about community and history, and about how human life survives in time:

> Refugees ask other refugees, who are we to come to you and who are you to come to us? Nobody answers. Palestinians, Syrians, Iraqis, Kurds share the camp, the same-different camp, the camp of a camp. They have all come to re-originate the beginning with their own hands and feet.[4]

For Arendt, 'Who are you?' is the question we address when we speak and act in the world. The actions involved in answering that question, she argues, are how we come together to grant one another the right to have rights, through our speech, our politics, our being together. Human rights in this sense, are never anything less—or more—than a community project. This is also why the answer to the question 'who are you?' invariably remains hidden from ourselves: essentially, it belongs to our lives with others. So too in Baddawi, in Qasmiyeh's poem, the question remains unanswered: 'Who are we and who are you?' 'Nobody answers.' This is not because questions of identity or community are unanswerable. Nobody answers for themselves because the history—the human time—that is being made in Baddawi, and the community at its heart, is being inaugurated, again and again, through the movement of people, with their own hands and feet.

Baddawi camp is thus always being written, for Qasmiyeh, in a process that quietly rips at the hearts of its new and old inhabitants. Each incarnation of the camp is born of a trauma and of the memory of trauma. Baddawi is also an archive of death, wounding, and mourning. This is not a metaphor. As Elena and Yousif explain in their photo-essay *The Absence of Paths* (exhibited as part of the 2017 Venice Biennale), the first threshold to be crossed in this place of multiple thresholds is the old cemetery (there used to be just one; a fifth was built in 2017).[5] You cannot avoid death in Baddawi if only because its cemetery is one of the very few horizontal spaces in the camp—a place where you can see in front of you. But to encounter death is also to encounter the refugee history that is continually re-making the camp: 'Born in Haifa in 1945... died in Baddawi in July 2016...Palestinian from Syria...' reads one tombstone. 'The words of—and over—the dead mark the multiple states of refugeeness, the past, and the place,' in Elena and Yousif's words.

Yet this constant historical presence—a memory that will not settle—is also why Qasmiyeh's poems insist again and again that 'the camp is time.' Like Arendt and Boochani (as we saw in the last chapter), Qasmiyeh is writing the time of survival into history. At the very least, this insistence on being in time is a direct challenge to the representation of refugee camps as ahistorical spaces of timeless—and agentless—suffering. As historians of humanitarianism have shown, the de-politicization of refugees' experience since the middle of the twentieth century has had the thoroughly political consequence of silencing, and in some cases—notably that of the Palestinians—obliterating, that history. By superseding the refugee camp of the humanitarian imaginary with the idea of a constantly written archive of refugee memory (the camp as time, not empty space), Qasmiyeh is also claiming the right to name the camp for generations of refugees, past and future: 'Only refugees can forever write the archive,' he writes: 'The camp owns the archive, not God':

> Only refugees can forever write the archive.
> The camp owns the archive, not God.
> For the archive not to fall apart, it weds the camp unceremoniously.
> The question of a camp-archive is also the question of the camp's survival beyond speech.[6]

The suppression of refugee history is an ideological constant in our current political culture. It as though refugees and migrants emerge through a mist by some quirk of bizarre bad luck, as though politics, policy, war, the climate emergency, and gross poverty had nothing to do with their suddenly being there on 'our' borders. By contrast, having nothing to lose, the rightless of Baddawi have no choice but to live with refugee history—more of it arrives daily. Because it cannot be pushed out, forgotten, banished, this archive of statelessness does something extraordinary:

it weaves a web, often silently, in the intangible—in a new sound, in the smell of new dishes, another knot of electricity wires, different footfalls—that holds the community of the camp together. It does this precariously, contingently but, by and large, in good faith and, since the withdrawal of UNRWA's (the UN organization established to provide humanitarian assistance for Palestinian refugees in 1949) funding by the Trump administration in 2018, increasingly dire circumstances.

'Refugees are Dialectical Beings' is the title of another poem. Again, Qasmiyeh is picking up on the phenomenology of Baddawi's changing landscape: the camp sounds different because the new refugees bring with them new dialects as a trace of their refugee history, of where they have come from, where they have been.[7] 'Haifa…1945…Palestinian from Syria.' 'The dialect that survives on its own is that of the dead,' Qasmiyeh writes: 'Dialects when uttered become spectres of time'. These dialects are also dialectical; they are same-different, other, threatening, uncanny, but also part of an on-going archive of refugeedom that is made and re-made by the arrival of each new accent: 'In dialects, we gather the ungathered with the subtlety of the dead,' the poem concludes. This is another characteristically dense line, but it compresses beautifully Qasmiyeh's vision of how the arrival of Syrian refugees to Baddawi traffics with the past, with the dead—with a long history of rightlessness—to gather a new community into being.

This is a political community lived in by citizen-refugees who are working, alongside those in other camps and migrant communities across the world, to maintain the non-state sovereignties necessary for people to live together. This is hardly utopian living; it is necessary living. But the avowal of what it means to be rightless is present in the warp and weft of Baddawi—its living-dead archive—does perhaps suggest some new imaginative terms for thinking about different models of citizenship and, possibly, different ways of thinking about rights. 'In writing about these events and others', Qasmiyeh has said in an interview with *Asympote Journal*, 'we chase the camps as if we were chasing ourselves in details that are no longer there to be observed transiently but to be inscribed and re-inscribed to create a new archive, that of the upcoming and the future.'[8] It is hard to think of a more fragile sense of being than to be chasing a history that is forever disappearing. Yet Qasmiyeh is still insisting here that a future archive for this history is possible. As Arendt said, there is still another way of writing history—and another way of writing the history of rights.

THE HANDS ARE HERS*

Yousif M. Qasmiyeh

The hands are hers—fractured urns of intimacy and anticipation.

They would cut, mend, darn, comb, bathe, clean, feel and above all submit themselves as seals of presence at the UNRWA distribution centres.

In this photograph, the face is outside the frame but the hands are certainly hers.

She is cutting runner beans, meticulously removing their fibrous ends and any impurities.

Her hands, the knife and the beans against the tin are the only elements in this landscape.

They all move in different directions and yet in total synchrony like a methodical machine.

The knife blade and the tin tray.

The hands and the beans.

The tray is the base, or more precisely the deathbed, for the fallen and everything perishable.

The hands are captured as close to and far from each other at the same time.

What is inextricable therein is sustained in the continuum of cutting, trimming and eventually the falling of the beans as singular and weakened parts.

The hands are certainly hers to the extent of complete dissolution and resurrection.

* First published by *Refugee Hosts*, 2018.

ENDNOTES

Preface and Acknowledgements

1. I am borrowing here from the title of Samuel Moyn's history of the material inequalities of modern human rights, *Not Enough: Human Rights in an Unequal World* (Cambridge, Mass.: Harvard University Press, 2018).
2. Susan Sontag, 'At the Same Time… (The Novelist and Moral Reasoning),' *English Studies in Africa* (2005), 48.1, pp. 5–17.
3. Hannah Arendt, *Lectures on Kant's Political Philosophy*, ed. Ronald Beiner (Chicago: University of Chicago Press, 1992), pp. 43–4.
4. See Michael Rothberg, *The Implicated Subject: Beyond Victims and Perpetrators* (Stanford, California: Stanford University Press, 2019).

Chapter One

1. Susan Marks, *Four Human Rights Myths*, 10, LSE Law, Society and Economy Working Papers, 8 (2012), 11, quoted in Joseph R. Slaughter, 'Hijacking Human Rights: Neoliberalism, the New Historiography, and the End of the Third World,' *Human Rights Quarterly*, 40(4), November 2018: p. 764.
2. Lynn Hunt, *Inventing Human Rights: A History* (New York: W.W. Norton, 2007).
3. Samuel Moyn, *The Last Utopia: Human Rights in History* (Cambridge, MA: Harvard, 2010).
4. See James Dawes, *Evil Men* (Cambridge, MA: Harvard University Press, 2013); Thomas Keenan, *Fables of Responsibility: Aberrations in Ethics and Politics* (Stanford, California: Stanford University Press, 1997); Bruce Robbins, *The Beneficiary* (Durham: Duke University Press, 2017); Richard Ashby Wilson and Richard D. Brown (eds.), *Humanitarianism and Suffering: The Mobilization of Empathy* (Cambridge: Cambridge University Pres, 2008); Joseph R. Slaughter, 'The Enchantment of Human Rights; or, What Difference Does Humanitarian Indifference

Make,' *Critical Quarterly*, December 2014, 56(4): pp. 46–67; Kay Schaffer and Sidonie Smith, *Human Rights and Narrated Lives: The Ethics of Recognition* (London: Palgrave, 2004); Elizabeth Anker, *Fictions of Dignity: Embodying Human Rights in World Literature* (Ithaca: Cornell University Press, 2012).

5. In October 2005, the Graduate Center at City University of New York held a major conference on the Humanities and Human Rights. The proceedings were published in the *PMLA*, 121(5), October 2006.

6. Crystal Parikh, 'Introduction,' in Parikh, C. (ed.) *The Cambridge Companion to Human Rights and Literature*, Cambridge: Cambridge University Press, 2018) pp. 1–9.

7. Richard McKeon, 'Philosophy and History in the Development of Human Rights,' in *Selected Writings of Richard McKeon: Philosophy, Science and Culture, Volume 1* (Chicago: Chicago University Press, 1998).

8. Martti Koskenniemi, 'Rights, History, Critique,' in *Human Rights: Moral or Political?*, ed. Adam Etinson (Oxford: Oxford University Press, 2018), p. 42.

9. Stephen Hopgood, *The Endtimes of Human Rights* (Ithaca, NY: Cornell University Press, 2013).

10. Hannah Arendt, 'Guests from No-Man's Land,' in *The Jewish Writings*, eds Jerome Kohn and Ron. H. Feldman (New York: Schocken Books, 2007), p. 211.

11. Jacques Rancière, 'Literary Communities,' in *The Common Growl: Towards a Poetics of Precarious Community*, ed. Thomas Claviez (New York: Fordham University Press, 2016), pp. 93–110.

12. According to the English Association, in the United Kingdom there has been a noted drop in the number of high-school students taking English Literature for their A-Level examinations (of up to about 25%) and a corresponding dip in the number of English Literature under-graduates. There are demographic issues that make this figure less dra-matic than it might appear, and some recent evidence suggests the decline may have levelled out. No ten-year standard deviation statistics were available at the time of writing. Similar kinds of decline in English enrolments have also been noted in the United States, although com-parative subject-specific statistics are more difficult to access. Data from the American Academy of Arts and Sciences suggests that English majors also declined around 25% between 2011 and 2017. But as Kyla Wazana Tompkins has pointed out, tellingly, in the same period,

applications in cultural, ethnic, and gender studies rose by 5%, suggesting that the issue here may not be simply the humanities, but what kinds of humanities and English majors are meeting the needs, desires, and aspirations of a diverse, and curious, generation of students. See Kyla Wazana Tompkins 'Are you OK Tobe White?', https://outoforder. substack.com/p/are-you-okay-tobe-white.

13. Rana Dajani, *We Love Reading*, https://welovereading.org.

14. Arundhati Roy, 'Peace and the New Corporate Liberation Theology,' *Sydney Morning Herald*, November 4, 2004, https://www.smh.com.au/ national/roys-full-speech-20041104-gdk1qn.html.

15. Salil Shetty, 'Decolonizing Human Rights,' Speech given at the London School of Economics, 22 May 2018, https://www.amnesty. org/download/Documents/DOC1084632018ENGLISH.pdf

16. Paul Bloom makes a cogent case against the overselling of empathy as a social and political good: *Against Empathy: The Case for Rational Compassion* (London: Bodley Head, 2017). For key analyses of the complexities of literary empathy see, *inter alia*, Elaine Scarry, 'The Difficulty of Imagining Other Persons,' *in The Handbook of Interethnic Coexistence*, ed. Eugene Weiner (New York: Continuum Publishing, 1998), pp. 40-62; Suzanne Keen, *Empathy and the Novel* (Oxford: Oxford University Press, 2007); and James Dawes, 'Human Rights, Literature, and Empathy', in *The Routledge Companion to Literature and Human Rights*, eds. Sophia A. McClennen and Alexandra Schultheis Moore (London and New York: Routledge, 2016), pp. 427–32.

17. Namwali Serpell, 'The Banality of Empathy', *The New York Review of Books*, March 2, 2019, https://www.nybooks.com/daily/2019/03/02/ the-banality-of-empathy/

18. Quoted in Robert Coles, 'James Baldwin is Home,' *The New York Times*, 31 July 1977, http://movies2.nytimes.com/books/98/03/29/specials/ baldwin-home.html.

19. Poetics, or *poiesis,* Srećko Horvat reminds us, following Marx in *Poetry from the Future* (2019), comes from the Greek verb,'*poeiein*, which means "to produce" in the sense of bringing something into being'. *Poetry from the Future* (London: Allen Lane, 2019), p. 130.

20. Behrouz Boochani, *No Friend but the Mountains* (2018), trans. Omid Tofighian (Picador: London, 2019), p. 209.

21. Primo Levi, *If This is a Man/The Truce* (1958/1963), trans. Stuart Woolf (London: Sphere Books, 1987), p. 35.

22. Itamar Mann, 'Boochani's Tribunal: Normalizing Human Degradation at the Borders,' *Just Security*, December 12, 2019, https://www.justsecurity.org/67718/boochanis-tribunal-normalizing-human-degradation-at-borders/

Chapter Two

1. Lionel Shriver, 'Fiction and Identity Politics', published in *The Guardian*, 13 September 2016, https://www.theguardian.com/commentisfree/2016/sep/13/lionel-shrivers-full-speech-i-hope-the-concept-of-cultural-appropriation-is-a-passing-fad.

2. Claudia Rankine, 'Why I'm spending $625,000 to Study Whiteness,' interview with Steven W. Thrasher, *The Guardian*, 19 October 2016, https://www.theguardian.com/books/2016/oct/19/claudia-rankine-macarthur-genius-grant-exploring-whiteness.

3. See Zadie Smith, 'Fascinated to Presume: In Defense of Fiction,' *The New York Review of Books*, October 24, 2019, https://www.nybooks.com/articles/2019/10/24/zadie-smith-in-defense-of-fiction/

4. Ian McEwan, 'Only Love and then Oblivion,' *The Guardian*, 15 September 2001, https://www.theguardian.com/world/2001/sep/15/september11.politicsphilosophyandsociety2.

5. Lynn Hunt, *Inventing Human Rights: A History*.

6. Quoted in Yogita Goyal, *Runaway Genres: The Global Afterlives of Slavery* (New York: New York University Press, 2019), p, 2.

7. James Chandler, *The Archaeology of Sympathy* (Chicago: Chicago University Press, 2013), p. xiv.

8. See Thomas L. Haskell, 'Capitalism and the Origins of the Humanitarian Sensibility', parts 1 and 2, *American Historical Review* 90 (1985): pp. 339–61, pp. 547–65.

9. Naomi Klein first made the connection between the rise of neo-liberalism and human rights in *The Shock Doctrine: The Rise of Disaster Capitalism* (London: Picador, 2008). See also Jessica Whyte, *The Morals of the Market: Human Rights and the Rise of Neo-Liberalism* (London: Verso, 2019).

10. Jean-Jacques Rousseau, *Émile, or An Education* (1762), trans. Barbara Foxley (London: Penguin, 1991), p. 173.

11. Daniel Defoe, *The Life and Adventures of Robinson Crusoe* (1719) (London: Penguin, 2004), p. 142.

12. See Lynn Festa, 'Humanity without Feathers,' *Humanity: An International Journal of Human Rights, Humanitarianism, and Development*, vol. 1 no. 1, 2010, pp. 3–27.

13. Wayne C. Booth, *A Rhetoric of Irony* (Chicago: Chicago University Press, 1974).

14. Jean-Jacques Rousseau, *Letter to d'Alembert and Writings for the Theater, The Collected Writings of Rousseau*, edited and translated by Allan Bloom, Charles Butterworth, and Christopher Kelly (Dartmouth: University Press of New England, 2004), p. 269.

15. Richard Rorty, *Contingency, Irony and Solidarity* (Cambridge: Cambridge University Press, 1993), p. 1.

16. Richard Rorty, 'Human Rights, Rationality, and Sentimentality,' *Truth and Progress: Philosophical Papers Volume 3* (Cambridge: Cambridge University Press, 1998), pp. 165–87.

17. Jean Paul Sartre, 'The Responsibility of the Writer', eds. David Hardman and Stephen Spender *Reflections on Our Age: Lectures Delivered at the Opening Session of UNESCO at the University of Paris*, (London: Allan Wingate, 1946), p. 68.

18. Sartre, 'Responsibility,' p. 70.

19. Milan Kundera, 'Jerusalem Address: The Novel and Europe' (1985) reprinted in *The Art of the Novel* (London: Faber, 1988), p. 157.

20. Brian Goodman, 'Human Rights as Antipolitics', presented at the Royal Irish Academy, Human Rights and Humanities Conference, Dublin, 7 December 2017.

21. Sartre, 'Responsibility', p. 168.

22. Rorty, *Contingency*, p. 82.

23. Rita Felski, *The Limits of Critique* (Chicago: Chicago University Press, 2015).

24. Quoted in Michael Ignatieff, *Human Rights as Politics and Idolatry* (Princeton, New Jersey: Princeton University Press, 2001), p. 80.

25. At the same time, a lot of energy and money was put into promoting cosmopolitan literary programmes by UNESCO and other cultural organizations with the aim of 're-humanizing' a public numbed by violence, occupation and fascism—and later also reassuring them about the values of Western culture just as writers, intellectuals, and politicians from de-colonizing countries were trying to draw attention to the fact that some histories of violence and occupation were not yet over, and that others were just beginning. See Sarah Brouillette,

UNESCO and the Fate of the Literary (Stanford, California: Stanford University Press, 2019).

26. Primo Levi, *If this is a Man* (1958) and *The Truce* (1963), trans. Stuart Woolf (London: Penguin, 1979), pp. 111–12.

27. Ignatieff, *Human Rights*, p. 4.

28. See Daniel Levy and Natan Sznaider, *Human Rights and Memory* (Pennsylvania: Pennsylvania State University Press, 2010).

29. Ignatieff, *Human Rights*, p. 4.

30. Joseph Slaughter, *Human Rights, Inc.* (New York: Fordham University Press, 2007), p. 48.

31. Johannes Morsink, *The Universal Declaration of Human Rights: Drafting, Origins and Intent* (Philadelphia: University of Pennsylvania Press, 2000).

32. Jessica Whyte, 'The Fortunes of Natural Man: Robinson Crusoe, Political Economy, and the Universal Declaration of Human Rights,' *Humanity: An International Journal of Human Rights, Humanitarianism, and Development*, 5(3), Winter 2014: 302.

33. Roland Burke, *Decolonization and the Evolution of International Human Rights* (Philadelphia: University of Pennsylvania Press, 2010).

34. Steven L. B. Jensen, *The Making of International Human Rights: The 1960s, Decolonization, and the Reconstruction of Global Values* (Cambridge: Cambridge University Press, 2016).

35. J M Coetzee, *Doubling the Point: Essays and Interviews*, ed. David Atwell (Boston: Harvard University. Press, 1992), p. 244.

36. My thanks to Anna Barnard for drawing my attention to the importance of these criticisms.

37. Kundera, 'Jerusalem Address', p. 157.

38. Mahmoud Darwish, *A Memory for Forgetfulness: Beirut, August 1982*, trans. Ibrahim Muhawi (Berkeley and Los Angeles: University of California Press, 2013).

39. Joseph Slaughter, 'Hijacking Human Rights: Neoliberalism, the New Historiography, and the End of the Third World,' *Human Rights Quarterly*, 40(4), November 2018: pp. 735–75.

40.. Hannah Arendt, '"The Rights of Man": What are They?', *The Modern Review* 3.1 (1949): pp. 4–37.

41. Hannah Arendt, *The Origins of Totalitarianism* (New York, Harcourt Books, 1994), p. 299.

42. See Hannah Arendt, 'Franz Kafka: A Revaluation' (1944), in *Essays in Understanding, 1930–1954: Formation, Exile and Totalitarianism*, ed. Jerome

Kohn (New York: Schocken, 1994), pp. 69–80, and 'Franz Kafka: Appreciated Anew' [originally published as 'Kafka, von neuem gewürdigt' (1946), trans. Martin Klebes, in *Reflections on Literature and Culture*, ed. by Susannah Young-ah Gottlieb (Stanford: Stanford University Press, 2007), pp. 94–109. I write about Arendt's reading of Kafka in terms of her evolving thinking about rights in 'Reading Statelessness: Arendt's Kafka,', *Placeless People: Writing, Rights, and Refugees* (Oxford: Oxford University Press, 2019), pp. 29–45.

43. Samuel Beckett, 'The End', *The Expelled, The Calmative, The End with First Love*, ed. Christopher Ricks, (London: Faber, 2009), p. 55. I've also written before about Beckett's anti-humanitarian post-war writing in 'Beckett's Expelled', in *Placeless People*, pp. 119–40.

44. Samuel Beckett, 'The Capital of the Ruins' (1946), in *The Complete Short Prose: 1929–1989*, ed. Stanley E. Gontarski (New York: Grove Press, 1995), pp. 275–8.

45. Theodor Adorno, 'Trying to Understand *Endgame*' (1961), *Notes to Literature, Volume 1* (New York: Columbia University Press, 1991), p. 244.

Chapter Three

1. Virginia Woolf, *Three Guineas* (1938), *A Room of One's Own* and *Three Guineas*, ed. Anna Snaith (Oxford: Oxford University Press, 2015), p. 215.

2. Susan Sontag, *Regarding the Pain of Others* (London: Hamish Hamilton, 2003), p. 5.

3. Caroline Brothers, *War and Photography* (London: Routledge, 1997).

4. Woolf, *Three Guineas*, p. 96.

5. Sontag, *Pain*, p. 6.

6. Woolf, *Three Guineas*, p. 90.

7. Woolf, *Three Guineas*, p. 119.

8. Woolf, *Three Guineas*, p. 151.

9. Woolf, *Three Guineas*, p. 156.

10. Woolf, *Three Guineas*, p. 179.

11. See Glenda Sluga, *Internationalism in the Age of Nationalism* (Philadelphia, Pennsylvania: University of Pennsylvania Press, 2013).

12. As Sluga notes 'bobbing alongside' a middle-class 'culture of international mindedness' within national norms, were demands 'for progress and liberty on an international scale 'on behalf of 'races as

well as classes, women as well as men' all 'those whom the nation had failed, and those who still waited the nation's arrival'. p. 65.

13. Woolf, *Three Guineas*, p. 185.
14. See Ravit Reichman, *The Affective Life of Law: Legal Modernism and the Literary Imagination* (Stanford: Stanford University Press, 2009).
15. See Rancière, 'Literary Communities'.
16. 'International Declaration of the Rights of Man,' October 12 1929, reprinted in Jacques Maritain, *Christianity and Democracy* (1943) and *The Rights of Man and The Natural Law* (1942), trans. Doris C. Anson (San Francisco: Ignatius Press, 2011), p. 139.
17. See Alexandre Lefebrve, *Human Rights and the Care of the Self* (Durham and London: Duke University Press, 2018).
18. Natasha Wheatley, 'Spectral Legal Personality in Interwar International Law: On New Ways of Not Being a State,' *Law and History Review,* 35 (3), 2017: pp. 753–87.
19. Nathaniel Berman, '"But the Alternative Is Despair": European Nationalism and the Modernist Renewal of International Law,' *Harvard Law Review,* 106 (8), 1993: p. 1832.
20. Hannah Arendt, '"The Rights of Man": What are They?,' p. 33.
21. Woolf, *Three Guineas*, p. 180.
22. Woolf, *Three Guineas*, p. 211.
23. Woolf, *Three Guineas*, p. 214.
24. Jacques Maritain, *The Rights of Man and The Natural Law*, p. 103.
25. Woolf, *Three Guineas*, p. 250.
26. Woolf's Antigone prefigures political philosopher Bonnie Honig's description of her interruptive politics and ethics. Bonnie Honig, *Antigone Interrupted* (Cambridge: Cambridge University Press, 2011).
27. See Honig as above; Judith Butler, *Antigone's Claim* (New York: Columbia University Press, 2002); Bracha L. Ettinger, *The Matrixial Border Space* (Minneapolis: University of Minnesota Press, 2006); and Luce Irigarary, *An Ethics of Sexual Difference* (Ithaca: Cornell University Press, 1993).
28. Every year the Aspen Institute in the United States brings leaders together to read, think, and ponder the questions of their time through the classics of world literature. Participants are required to stage a version of *Antigone*. One year, the future US Secretary of State Madeline Albright took the title role. See Linda Kunstler, 'Inside Aspen: the mountain retreat for the liberal elite,' *The Economist, 1843,* October/ November 2019, https://www.1843magazine.com/features/inside-aspen-the-mountain-retreat-for-the-liberal-elite.

29. Simone Weil, 'Human Personality,' (1950), written between 1942 and 1943, reprinted in *Simone Weil: An Anthology*, ed. Siân Mills (London: Penguin, 2005), p. 83.

30. Weil, 'Human Personality,' p. 86.

31. See Suzanne Césaire, 'The Great Camouflage', *Tropiques* 13–14 (1945) and 'Surrealism and Us,' *Tropiques* 8–9 (1943): 37, both. reprinted in *The Great Camouflage: The Writings of Dissent, 1941–1945*, ed. Daniel Maximin, trans. Keith L. Walker (Connecticut: Wesleyan University Press, 2012).

32. Weil, 'The Power of Words,' (1937), reprinted in *Simone Weil: An Anthology*, p. 245.

33. Weil, 'The Power of Words,' p. 298.

Chapter Four

1. Mahbubeh Jamal Vatan, testimony to Royal Borough of Kensington and Chelsea Council, trans. © Kayvan Tahmasebian. The testimonies of survivors and citizens are not recorded in the official minutes. However, the livestream of the meeting can be found on the RBKC website: https://www.youtube.com/watch?v=I8mpvkPLpoI&feature=youtu.be (accessed 31 October 2019)

2. Translated by Homa Katouzian, *Saadi: The Poet of Life, Love and Compassion* (Oxford: Oneworld Publications, 2006), p. 31.

3. Édouard Glissant, *Poetics of Relation*, trans. Betsy Wing (Ann Arbour: University of Michigan Press, 1997), p. 9.

4. Ben Okri, 'Grenfell Tower, June 2017,' *Channel Four News*, broadcast 26 June 2017: https://www.channel4.com/news/ben-okri-on-grenfell-tower-you-catch-the-fever-of-that-anger.

5. Ben Okri, 'Active Citizenship', Word Factory Citizen Festival, 2017, reprinted in the *Guardian*, 30 January 2018, https://www.theguardian.com/commentisfree/2018/jan/30/populism-brexit-citizens-political-responsibility?CMP=share_btn_tw

6. The 'Ghosts of Grenfell' was the title of a multi-voiced epic song released later that summer by the musician and political activist, Lowkey. The song listed the names of all seventy-two victims in a direct address to the royal borough of Kensington and Chelsea: 'To whom it may concern,/ at the Queen's Royal Borough of Kensington in Chelsea ... Where are all these people?' It may not, of course—and this was Lowkey's point—concern those at the borough at all, at least in any meaningful way, if they cannot see who or what it is they are being

asked to show concern for. 'The only ghosts are us' runs another line. See Lowkey, 'Ghosts of Grenfell', featuring Mai Khalil, August 2017: https://www.youtube.com/watch?v=ztUamrChczQ.

7. By contrast, many citizens in Kensington and Chelsea live on a permanent upgrade: this is the richest local borough council in the United Kingdom. The average annual wage is £65,000 (roughly $85,000).

8. For an account of how the figure of the ultimate 'victim devoid of agency' helped develop cosmopolitan human rights following the Holocaust, see Daniel Levy and Natan Sznaider, *Human Rights and Memory.*

9. Étienne Balibar, *Citizenship*, trans. Thomas Scott-Railton (Cambridge: Polity, 2015), p. 31.

10. Hannah Arendt, *Eichmann in Jerusalem: A Report on the Banality of Evil* (1963) (London: Penguin, 1994), p. 49.

11. Daniel Renwick, 'Organising on Mute,' in *After Grenfell: Violence, Resistance and Response*, eds. Dan Bulley, Jenny Edkins and Nadine El-Enany (London: Pluto Press, 2019), pp. 19–46.

12. Leila Fahra, 'UK May have breached Human Rights', 9 March 2018, *The Guardian*, https://www.theguardian.com/uk-news/2018/mar/09/grenfell-tower-uk-may-have-breached-human-rights-says-un.

13. Arendt first used this phrase in 1949 just after the UDHR was adopted ('"The Rights of Man": What are They?')

14. Hannah Arendt, 'We Refugees' (1943), in *The Jewish Writings*, eds. Jerome Kohn and Ron H. Feldman (New York: Shocken Books, 2007), pp. 264–74.

15. Minutes of a meeting of the Council Held on 19 July 2017 at the Town Hall, Hornton Street, London, W6 7HX, https://www.rbkc.gov.uk/committees/Home.aspx.

16. Paul Ricœur, *The Rule of Metaphor: Multi-disciplinary Studies of the Creation of Meaning in Language*, (Toronto: University of Toronto Press, 1977), p. 224.

17. Balibar, *Citizenship*, p. 7.

18. Saadi Shirazi, *The Gulistan of Saadi Shirazi*, trans. Edward Rehatsek, eds. Reza Nazari and Somayeh Nazari, (CreateSpace Independent Publishing Platform, 2016), pp. 79–81.

19. Quoted Katouzian, *Saadi*, p. 8

20. John Donne, 'Meditation XVII', *Devotions on Emergent Occasions, John Donne: Collected Poetry*, ed. Christopher Ricks (London: Penguin, 2012), p. 314.

Chapter Five

1. Kamila Shamsie, *Home Fire* (London: Bloomsbury 2017), p. 259.
2. 'Shamima Begum: ISIS bride's face used as target at Merseyside shooting range', *The Independent*, 27 February 2019, https://www.independent.co.uk/news/uk/home-news/shamima-begum-isis-bride-shooting-range-gun-merseyside-a8799326.html (accessed 12 July 2019)
3. Sigmund Freud, "Thoughts for the Times on War and Death." (1915). *The Standard Edition*, Vol. 14, p. 275.
4. Freud, 'Thoughts', p. 277.
5. Arendt, *On Violence* (New York, 1970).
6. Balibar, *Citizenship*, p. 73.
7. Kamila Shamsie, 'Exiled: The Disturbing Story of a Citizen Made UnBritish', *The Guardian*, 1November 2018, https://www.theguardian.com/books/2018/nov/17/unbecoming-british-kamila-shamsie-citizens-exile.
8. See Shaheed Fatima, 'Citizenship-Stripping and ISIS Members: The Recent UK Experience, *Just Security*, March 11 2019, https://www.justsecurity.org/63164/citizenship-stripping-isis-members-uk-united-kingdom-bangladesh-britain-experience-shamima-begum/ (accessed 12 July 2019) and Farhaan Uddin, 'Shamima Begum may be a Bangladeshi Citizen After All', *EJIL: Talk!*, March 14 2019, https://www.ejiltalk.org/shamima-begum-may-be-a-bangladeshi-citizen-after-all/ (accessed 12 July 2019).
9. Robert M. Cover, 'Violence and the Word' (1986) reprinted in *On Violence: A Reader*, eds. Bruce B. Lawrence and Aisha Karim (Durham: 2007), p. 295.
10. Ankhi Mukherjee, 'On Antigone's Suffering', unpublished paper, MLA, Seattle, January 2020, forthcoming in *The Cambridge Journal of Postcolonial Literary Inquiry*.
11. Shamsie, *Home Fire*, p. 260.
12. Shamsie, *Home Fire*, p. 171.

Chapter Six

1. Chris Abani, 'The Road' in *The Displaced: Refugee Writers on Refugee Lives*, ed. Viet Thanh Nguyen (Abrams: New York, 2019), p. 25.
2. Aleksander Hemon, 'God's Fate' in *The Displaced*, p. 100.

3. Today relatively few people fall into the strict legal category of statelessness, compared to looser definitions of who counts as a refugee or asylum seeker. I use 'statelessness' to refer to the historical and existential condition of statelessness that in legal and political terms menaces both the displaced and defensive paranoia of those who fear and condemn them.

4. Ernest Renan, 'What is a Nation?' trans. Martin Thom, in *Nation and Narration*, ed. Homi K. Bhabha (New York: Routledge, 1990), pp. 8–22. See also Homi K. Bhabha's classic essay, 'DissemiNation: Time, Narrative, and the Margins of the Modern Nation', in *The Location of Culture* (London: Routledge, 1994), pp. 199–244.

5. Ian Baucom, 'Afterword: States of Time', *Contemporary Literature*, 49(4), Winter 2008: p. 713.

6. Baucom 'Afterword', p. 714.

7. Gary Wilder, *Freedom Time: Negritude, Decolonization, and the Future of the World* (Durham: Duke University Press, 2015).

8. Hannah Arendt, *The Origins of Totalitarianism* (1951) (Harcourt, Brace, Jovanovich: New York, 1973), p. 299.

9. For an indispensable reading of Arendt's critique of sovereignty, see Dana Villa, *Arendt and Heidegger: The Fate of the Political* (New Jersey, 1996).

10. Arendt, *Origins*, p. 296.

11. Arendt, 'What is Freedom?' in *Between Past and Future* (London: Penguin, 1993), pp. 164–5.

12. Paul Ricœur, 'Action, Story and History: Re-reading *The Human Condition*,' *Salmagundi*, No. 60, On Hannah Arendt (Spring-Summer 1983): p. 60.

13. See Paul Ricœur, *Time and Narrative, Volume 3*, trans. Kathleen Blamey and David Pellauer (University of Chicago Press: Chicago, 1988).

14. Behrouz Boochani, *No Friend But the Mountains* (2018), trans. Omid Tofighian (Picador: London, 2019), p. 191.

15. Ricœur, 'Action,' p. 65.

16. Hannah Arendt, *The Human Condition* (1958) (Chicago University Press: Chicago, 1998), p. 184.

17. Lyndsey Stonebridge, 'Hannah Arendt in Baddawi' in *Sovereignty in a Global Perspective*, ed. Christopher Smith (British Academy Publications: London, forthcoming).

18. Arendt, *Human Condition*, p. 208.

19. Arendt, *Human Condition*, p. 236.
20. Arendt, 'The Concept of History', *Between Past and Future* p. 47.
21. Arendt, 'The Concept of History', p. 87.
22. Arendt, 'The Concept of History', p. 67.
23. Quoted Arendt, 'The Concept of History,' n. 285.
24. Boochani, *No Friend*, p. 165.
25. Boochani, *No Friend*, p. 27.
26. Boochani, *No Friend*, p. 38.
27. Omid Tofighian, 'No Friend but the Mountains: Translator's Reflections,' in Boochani, *No Friend*, pp. 366–7.
28. Edward Said, 'Reflections on Exile,' *Reflections on Exile and Other Essays* (London: Granta, 2001), p. 180.
29. Elena Fiddian-Qasmiyeh, 'The Poetics of Undisclosed Care', *Refugee Hosts*, https://refugeehosts.org/2019/05/21/the-poetics-of-undisclosed-care/ accessed 20 August 2019.
30. Boochani, *No Friend*, p. 36.
31. Boochani, *No Friend*, p. 247.
32. Boochani, *No Friend*, p. 112.
33. Boochani, *No Friend*, p. 347.

Chapter Seven

1. Hannah Arendt, 'Political Experiences in the Twentieth Century,' Lectures—1969, The Hannah Arendt Papers at the Library of Congress: https://memory.loc.gov/cgi-bin/ampage?collId=mharendt_pub&fileName=04/040490/040490page.db&recNum=1&itemLink=/ammem/arendthtml/mharendtFolderP04.html&linkText=7
2. For blogs, creative work, and research-in-progress, see *Refugee Hosts*, https://refugeehosts.org.
3. Elena Fiddian-Qasmiyeh, 'The Poetics of Undisclosed Care', *Refugee Hosts*, https://refugeehosts.org/2019/05/21/the-poetics-of-undisclosed-care/.
4. Yousif M. Qasmiyeh, 'Vis-à-Vis or a Camp', https://refugeehosts.org/2016/09/30/writing-the-camp/
5. Elena Fiddian-Qasmiyeh and Yousif M. Qasmiyeh, 'The Absence of Paths', http://www.theabsenceofpaths.com/commission/at-the-core-of-the-badawwi-camp
6. Yousif M. Qasmiyeh, 'Writing the camp archive', https://refugeehosts.org/2016/09/30/writing-the-camp/

7. Yousif M. Qasmiyeh, 'Refugees are Dialectical Beings,' https://
refugeehosts.org/2017/09/01/refugees-are-dialectical-beings-part-one/
8. Theophilus Kwek, 'In Conversation: Yousif M. Qasmiyeh on
Language and Liminality,' *Asympotote*, February 15 2017. https://www.
asymptotejournal.com/blog/2017/02/15/in-conversation-yousif-m-
qasmiyeh-on-language-and-liminality/

BIBLIOGRAPHY

Abani, C., 'The Road' in *The Displaced: Refugee Writers on Refugee Lives*, ed. Viet Thanh Nguyen (Abrams: New York, 2019).

Adorno, T., 'Trying to Understand *Endgame*' (1961), *Notes to Literature, Volume 1* (New York: Columbia University Press, 1991).

Anker, E., *Fictions of Dignity: Embodying Human Rights in World Literature* (Ithaca: Cornell University Press, 2012).

Arendt, A., 'We Refugees' (1943), in *The Jewish Writings*, eds. Jerome Kohn and Ron H. Feldman (New York: Shocken Books, 2007), pp. 264–74.

Arendt, H., 'Franz Kafka: A Revaluation' (1944), in *Essays in Understanding, 1930–1954: Formation, Exile and Totalitarianism*, ed. Jerome Kohn (New York: Schocken, 1994), pp. 69–80.

Arendt, H., 'Franz Kafka: Appreciated Anew' [originally published as 'Kafka, von neuem gewürdigt'] (1946), trans. Martin Klebes, in *Reflections on Literature and Culture*, ed. Susannah Young-ah Gottlieb (Stanford: Stanford University Press, 2007), pp. 94–109.

Arendt, H., '"The Rights of Man": What are They?' *The Modern Review* 3(1), 1949.

Arendt, H., 'Political Experiences in the Twentieth Century,' Lectures—1969, The Hannah Arendt Papers at the Library of Congress: https://memory. loc.gov/cgi-bin/ampage?collId=mharendt_pub&fileName=04/040490/ 040490page.db&recNum=1&itemLink=/ammem/arendthtml/ mharendtFolderP04.html&linkText=7.

Arendt, H., *The Origins of Totalitarianism* (1951) (New York: Schocken Books, 1994).

Arendt, H., *Lectures on Kant's Political Philosophy*, ed. Ronald Beiner (Chicago: University of Chicago Press, 1992).

Arendt, H., 'What is Freedom?' in *Between Past and Future* (London: Penguin, 1993).

Arendt, H., *Eichmann in Jerusalem: A Report on the Banality of Evil* (London: Penguin, 1963/1994).

Arendt, H., *The Human Condition* (1958) (Chicago University Press: Chicago, 1998).

Arendt, H., 'Guests from No-Man's Land,' in *The Jewish Writings*, eds. Jerome Kohn and Ron. H. Feldman (New York: Schocken Books, 2007).

Balibar, É., *Citizenship*, trans. Thomas Scott-Railton (Cambridge: Polity, 2015).

Baucom, I., 'Afterword: States of Time', *Contemporary Literature*, 49(4), Winter 2008: 712–17.

Beckett, S., 'The Capital of the Ruins' (1946), in *The Complete Short Prose: 1929–1989*, ed. Stanley E. Gontarski (New York: Grove Press, 1995), pp. 275–8.

Beckett, S., 'The End', *The Expelled, The Calmative, The End with First Love*, ed. Christopher Ricks, (London: Faber, 2009).

Berman, N., ' "But the Alternative Is Despair": European Nationalism and the Modernist Renewal of International Law,' *Harvard Law Review*, 106 (8), 1993: 1792–1903.

Bloom, P., *Against Empathy: The Case for Rational Compassion* (London: Bodley Head, 2017).

Boochani, B., *No Friend but the Mountains* (2018), trans. Omid Tofighian (Picador: London, 2019).

Booth, W.C., *A Rhetoric of Irony* (Chicago: Chicago University Press, 1974).

Brothers, C., *War and Photography* (London: Routledge, 1997).

Brouillette, S., *UNESCO and the Fate of the Literary* (Stanford: Stanford University Press, 2019).

Burke, R., *Decolonization and the Evolution of International Human Rights* (Philadelphia: University of Pennsylvania Press, 2010).

Butler, J., *Antigone's Claim* (New York: Columbia University Press, 2002).

Césaire, S., 'The Great Camouflage', *Tropiques* 13–14 (1945) and 'Surrealism and Us,' *Tropiques* 8–9 (1943): 37, both. reprinted in *The Great Camouflage: The Writings of Dissent, 1941–1945*, ed. Daniel Maximin, trans. Keith L. Walker (Connecticut: Wesleyan University Press, 2012).

Chandler, J., *The Archaeology of Sympathy* (Chicago: Chicago University Press, 2013).

Coetzee, J. M., *Doubling the Point: Essays and Interviews*, ed. David Atwell (Boston: Harvard University. Press, 1992).

Cover, R. M., 'Violence and the Word' (1986) reprinted in *On Violence: A Reader*, eds. Bruce B. Lawrence and Aisha Karim (Durham: Duke University Press, 2007).

Dajani, R. *We Love Reading*, https://welovereading.org.

Darwish, M., *A Memory for Forgetfulness: Beirut, August 1982*, trans. Ibrahim Muhawi (Berkeley and Los Angeles: University of California Press, 2013).

Dawes, J., *Evil Men* (Cambridge, MA: Harvard University Press, 2013).

Dawes, J., 'Human Rights, Literature, and Empathy' *The Routledge Companion to Literature and Human Rights*, eds. Sophia A. McClennen and Alexandra Schultheis Moore (London and New York: Routledge, 2016), pp. 427–32.

Defoe, D., *The Life and Adventures of Robinson Crusoe* (1719) (London: Penguin, 2004).

Donne, J., 'Meditation XVII', *Devotions on Emergent Occasions, John Donne: Collected Poetry*, ed. Christopher Ricks (London: Penguin, 2012).

Ettinger, B. L., *The Matrixial Border Space* (Minneapolis: University of Minnesota Press, 2006).

Fahra, L., 'UK May Have Breached Human Rights', 9 March 2018, *The Guardian*, https://www.theguardian.com/uk-news/2018/mar/09/grenfell-tower-uk-may-have-breached-human-rights-says-un.

Fatima, S., 'Citizenship-Stripping and ISIS Members: The Recent UK Experience, *Just Security*, March 11 2019, https://www.justsecurity.org/63164/citizenship-stripping-isis-members-uk-united-kingdom-bangladesh-britain-experience-shamima-begum/.

Felski, R., *The Limits of Critique* (Chicago: Chicago University Press, 2015).

Festa, L., 'Humanity without Feathers,' *Humanity: An International Journal of Human Rights, Humanitarianism, and Development*, vol. 1 no. 1, 2010, 3–27.

Fiddian-Qasmiyeh, E., 'The Poetics of Undisclosed Care', *Refugee Hosts*, https://refugeehosts.org/2019/05/21/the-poetics-of-undisclosed-care/.

Fiddian-Qasmiyeh, E. and Qasmiyeh, Y. M., 'The Absence of Paths', http://www.theabsenceofpaths.com/commission/at-the-core-of-the-badawwi-camp

Freud, S., 'Thoughts for the Times on War and Death.' (1915). *The Standard Edition*, Vol. 14.

Glissant, E., *Poetics of Relation*, trans. Betsy Wing (Ann Arbour: University of Michigan Press, 1997).

Goodman, B., 'Human Rights as Antipolitics', presented at the Royal Irish Academy, Human Rights and Humanities Conference, Dublin, 7 December 2017.

Goyal, Y. *Runaway Genres: The Global Afterlives of Slavery* (New York: New York University Press, 2019).

Haskell, T. L., 'Capitalism and the Origins of the Humanitarian Sensibility', parts 1 and 2, *American Historical Review* 90 (1985): 339–61, 547–65.

Honig, B., *Antigone Interrupted* (Cambridge: Cambridge University Press, 2011).

Hopgood, S., *The Endtimes of Human Rights* (Ithaca, NY: Cornell University Press, 2013).

Horvat, S., *Poetry from the Future* (London: Allen Lane, 2019).

Hunt, L., *Inventing Human Rights: A History* (New York: W.W. Norton, 2007).

Ignatieff, M., *Human Rights as Politics and Idolatry* (Princeton, New Jersey: Princeton University Press, 2001).

Irigarary, L., *An Ethics of Sexual Difference* (Ithaca: Cornell University Press, 1993).

Jensen, S. L. B., *The Making of International Human Rights: The 1960s, Decolonization, and the Reconstruction of Global Values* (Cambridge: Cambridge University Press, 2016).

Keen, S., *Empathy and the Novel* (Oxford: Oxford University Press, 2007).

Keenan, T., *Fables of Responsibility: Aberrations in Ethics and Politics* (Stanford: Stanford University Press, 1997).

Klein, N., *The Shock Doctrine: The Rise of Disaster Capitalism* (London: Picador, 2008).

Koskenniemi, M., 'Rights, History, Critique,' in *Human Rights: Moral or Political?*, ed. Adam Etinson (Oxford: Oxford University Press, 2018).

Katouzian, H. (trans.), *Saadi: The Poet of Life, Love and Compassion* (Oxford: Oneworld Publications, 2006).

Kundera, M., 'Jerusalem Address: The Novel and Europe' (1985) reprinted in *The Art of the Novel* (London: Faber, 1988).

Kunstler, L., 'Inside Aspen: The Mountain Retreat for the Liberal Elite,' *The Economist, 1843*, October/November 2019, https://www.1843magazine.com/features/inside-aspen-the-mountain-retreat-for-the-liberal-elite.

Kwek, T., 'In Conversation: Yousif M. Qasmiyeh on Language and Liminality,' *Asympotote*, February 15 2017, https://www.asymptotejournal.com/blog/2017/02/15/in-conversation-yousif-m-qasmiyeh-on-language-and-liminality/.

Lefebrve, A., *Human Rights and the Care of the Self* (Durham: Duke University Press, 2018).

Levi, P., *If This is a Man/The Truce* (1958/1963), trans. Stuart Woolf (London: Sphere Books, 1987).

Levy, D. and Sznaider, N., *Human Rights and Memory* (Pennsylvania: Pennsylvania State University. Press, 2010).

Lowkey, 'Ghosts of Grenfell', featuring Mai Khalil, August 2017: https://www.youtube.com/watch?v=ztUamrChczQ.

Mann, I. 'Boochani's Tribunal: Normalizing Human Degradation at the Borders,' *Just Security*, December 12, 2019, https://www.justsecurity. org/67718/boochanis-tribunal-normalizing-human-degradation-at-borders/.

Maritain, J., *Christianity and Democracy* (1943) and *The Rights of Man and The Natural Law* (1942), trans. Doris C. Anson (San Francisco: Ignatius Press, 2011).

McEwan, I., 'Only Love and then Oblivion,' *The Guardian*, 15 September 2001, https://www.theguardian.com/world/2001/sep/15/september11. politicsphilosophyandsociety2.

McKeon, R. 'Philosophy and History in the Development of Human Rights,' in *Selected Writings of Richard McKeon: Philosophy, Science and Culture, volume 1* (Chicago: Chicago University Press, 1998).

Morsink, J., *The Universal Declaration of Human Rights: Drafting, Origins and Intent* (Philadelphia: University of Pennsylvania Press, 2000).

Moyn, S., *The Last Utopia: Human Rights in History* (Cambridge, MA: Harvard, 2010).

Moyn, S., *Not Enough: Human Rights in an Unequal World* (Cambridge, Mass.: Harvard University Press, 2018).

Mukherjee, A., 'On Antigone's Suffering', delivered MLA, Seattle, January 2020, forthcoming in *Cambridge Journal of Postcolonial Literary Inquiry*.

Okri, B., 'Grenfell Tower, June 2017,' *Channel Four News*, broadcast 26 June 2017: https://www.channel4.com/news/ben-okri-on-grenfell-tower-you-catch-the-fever-of-that-anger.

Okri, B., 'Active Citizenship', Word Factory Citizen Festival, 2017, reprinted in the *Guardian*, 30 January 2018, https://www.theguardian.com/commentisfree/2018/jan/30/populism-brexit-citizens-political-responsibility?CMP=share_btn_tw.

Parikh, Crystal, 'Introduction,' in Parikh, C. (ed.) *The Cambridge Companion to Human Rights and Literature*, Cambridge: Cambridge University Press, 2018).

Qasmiyeh, Y. M., 'Vis-à-Vis or a Camp', https://refugeehosts.org/2016/09/30/writing-the-camp/

Qasmiyeh, Y. M., 'Writing the Camp Archive', https://refugeehosts. org/2016/09/30/writing-the-camp/

Qasmiyeh, Y. M., 'Refugees are Dialectical Beings,' https://refugeehosts. org/2017/09/01/refugees-are-dialectical-beings-part-one/.

Rancière, J., 'Literary Communities,' in *The Common Growl: Towards a Poetics of Precarious Community*, ed. Thomas Claviez (New York: Fordham University Press, 2016), pp. 93–110.

Rankine, C., 'Why I'm spending $625,000 to Study Whiteness,' interview with Steven W. Thrasher, *The Guardian*, 19 October 2016, https://www.theguardian.com/books/2016/oct/19/claudia-rankine-macarthur-genius-grant-exploring-whiteness.

Renan, E., 'What is a Nation?' trans. Martin Thom, in *Nation and Narration*, ed. Homi K. Bhabha (New York: Routledge, 1990), pp. 8–22.

Reichman, R., *The Affective Life of Law: Legal Modernism and the Literary Imagination* (Stanford: Stanford University Press, 2009).

Renwick, D., 'Organising on Mute,' in *After Grenfell: Violence, Resistance and Response*, eds. Dan Bulley, Jenny Edkins and Nadine El-Enany (London: Pluto Press, 2019).

Ricœur, P., *The Rule of Metaphor: Multi-Disciplinary Studies of the Creation of Meaning in Language* (Toronto: University of Toronto Press, 1977).

Ricœur, P., 'Action, Story and History: Re-Reading *the Human Condition*,' *Salmagundi*, No. 60, On Hannah Arendt (Spring-Summer 1983): 60–72.

Ricœur, P., *Time and Narrative, Volume 3*, trans. Kathleen Blamey and David Pellauer (University of Chicago Press: Chicago, 1988).

Rorty, R., *Contingency, Irony and Solidarity* (Cambridge: Cambridge University Press, 1993).

Rorty, R., 'Human Rights, Rationality, and Sentimentality,' *Truth and Progress: Philosophical Papers Volume 3* (Cambridge: Cambridge University Press, 1998).

Rothberg, M., *The Implicated Subject: Beyond Victims and Perpetrators* (Stanford: Stanford University Press, 2019).

Rousseau, J. J., *Émile, or an Education* (1762), trans. Barbara Foxley (London: Penguin, 1991).

Roy, A., 'Peace and the New Corporate Liberation Theology,' *Sydney Morning Herald*, November 4, 2004, https://www.smh.com.au/national/roys-full-speech-20041104-gdk1qn.html.

Said, E., 'Reflections on Exile,' *Reflections on Exile and Other Essays* (London: Granta, 2001).

Sartre, J. P., 'The Responsibility of the Writer', *Reflections on Our Age: Lectures Delivered at the Opening Session of UNESCO At The University of Paris*, eds. David Hardman and Stephen Spender (London: Allan Wingate, 1946).

Scarry, E., 'The Difficulty of Imagining Other Persons,' in *The Handbook of Interethnic Coexistence*, ed. Eugene Weiner (New York: Continuum Publishing, 1998), 40–62.

Schaffer, Kay J. R. and Smith, S., *Human Rights and Narrated Lives: The Ethics of Recognition* (London: Palgrave, 2004).

Serpell, N., 'The Banality of Empathy', *The New York Review of Books*, March 2, 2019, https://www.nybooks.com/daily/2019/03/02/the-banality-of-empathy/.

Shamsie, K., *Home Fire* (London: Bloomsbury 2017).

Shamsie, K., 'Exiled: The Disturbing Story of a Citizen Made Unbritish', *The Guardian*, 17 November 2018, https://www.theguardian.com/books/2018/nov/17/unbecoming-british-kamila-shamsie-citizens-exile.

Shetty, S., 'Decolonizing Human Rights,' Speech given at the London School of Economics, 22 May 2018, https://www.amnesty.org/download/Documents/DOC1084632018ENGLISH.pdf.

Sa'di, S., *The Gulistan of Saadi Shirazi*, trans. Edward Rehatsek, eds. Reza Nazari and Somayeh Nazari, (CreateSpace Independent Publishing Platform, 2016).

Shriver, L., 'Fiction and Identity Politics', published in *The Guardian*, 13 September 2016, https://www.theguardian.com/commentisfree/2016/sep/13/lionel-shrivers-full-speech-i-hope-the-concept-of-cultural-appropriation-is-a-passing-fad.

Slaughter, J., *Human Rights, Inc.* (New York: Fordham University Press, 2007).

Slaughter, J. R., 'The Enchantment Of Human Rights; Or, What Difference does Humanitarian Indifference Make,' *Critical Quarterly*, December 2014, 56(4): 46–67.

Slaughter, J. R., 'Hijacking Human Rights: Neoliberalism, the New Historiography, and the End of the Third World,' *Human Rights Quarterly*, 40(4), November 2018: 735–75.

Sluga, G., *Internationalism in the Age of Nationalism* (Philadelphia, Pennsylvania: University of Pennsylvania Press, 2013).

Smith, Z., 'Fascinated to Presume: In Defense of Fiction,' *The New York Review of Books*, October 24, 2019, https://www.nybooks.com/articles/2019/10/24/zadie-smith-in-defense-of-fiction/.

Sontag, S., *Regarding the Pain of Others* (London: Hamish Hamilton, 2003).

Sontag, S., 'At the Same Time...(The Novelist and Moral Reasoning),' *English Studies in Africa* (2005), 48.1, pp. 5–17.

Stonebridge, L., *Placeless People: Writing, Rights, and Refugees* (Oxford: Oxford University Press, 2019).

Stonebridge, L., '"The definite is the shadow and not the owner": Hannah Arendt in the shadows of sovereignty' in *Sovereignty in a Global Perspective*, ed. Christopher Smith (British Academy Publications: London, forthcoming).

Uddin, F., 'Shamima Begum may be a Bangladeshi Citizen After All', *EJIL: Talk!*, March 14 2019, https://www.ejiltalk.org/shamima-begum-may-be-a-bangladeshi-citizen-after-all/.

Vatan, M. J., Testimony to Royal Borough of Kensington and Chelsea Council, trans. Kayvan Tahmasebian. https://www.youtube.com/watch?v=I8mpvkPLpoI&feature=youtu.be (accessed 31 October 2019).

Villa, D., *Arendt and Heidegger: The Fate of the Political* (New Jersey, 1996).

Wazana Tompkins, K. 'Are you OK Tobe White?', https://outoforder.substack.com/p/are-you-okay-tobe-white.

Weil, S., 'Human Personality,' (1950), reprinted in *Simone Weil: An Anthology*, ed. Siân Mills (London: Penguin, 2005).

Wheatley, N., 'Spectral Legal Personality in Interwar International Law: On New Ways of Not Being a State,' *Law and History Review*, 35 (3), 2017: 753–87.

Whyte, J., 'The Fortunes of Natural Man: Robinson Crusoe, Political Economy, and the Universal Declaration of Human Rights,' *Humanity: An International Journal of Human Rights, Humanitarianism, and Development*, 5(3), Winter 2014.

Whyte, J., *The Morals of the Market: Human Rights and the Rise of Neo-Liberalism* (London: Verso, 2019).

Wilder, G., *Freedom Time: Negritude, Decolonization, and the Future of the World* (Durham: Duke University Press, 2015).

Wilson, R. Ashby and Brown, R. D. Brown (eds.), *Humanitarianism and Suffering: The Mobilization of Empathy* (Cambridge: Cambridge University Press, 2008).

Woolf, V., *Three Guineas* (1938), A *Room of One's Own* and *Three Guineas*, ed. Anna Snaith (Oxford: Oxford University Press, 2015).

INDEX

For the benefit of digital users, indexed terms that span two pages (e.g., 52–53) may, on occasion, appear on only one of those pages.